CORNELL STUDIES IN ANTHROPOLOGY

RELUCTANT PIONEERS
Village Development in Israel

Cornell Studies in Anthropology

This series of publications seeks particularly to provide descriptive accounts and interpretations of cultural process and dynamics, including those involved in projects of planned cultural change, among diverse cultures of the world.

Reluctant Pioneers

Village Development in Israel

By ALEX WEINGROD

Cornell University Press

ITHACA, NEW YORK

CORNELL UNIVERSITY PRESS

First published 1966

Library of Congress Catalog Card Number: 66-13648

PRINTED AND BOUND IN THE UNITED STATES OF AMERICA
BY VAIL-BALLOU PRESS, INC.

For my parents

Preface

WHY "reluctant pioneers"? The title indicates some of the ironies stemming from the emigration of Moroccan Jews to Israel and their settlement there in small villages.

This study primarily concerns a single village, a place that I call Oren. Oren is situated in Israel's southland, the Negev. Historically, the Negev has been a relatively barren, sparsely populated semidesert. To the European Jews who migrated to Palestine in the first half of this century, the Negev was a hope and a challenge. It was the desert that might be redeemed, a barren region that could, with toil and care, become a home for thousands of new Jewish farmers. The Negev represented pioneering, and those who went to live there were fulfilling the high ideals of national and personal transformation.

This book, however, is a study of immigrants from Morocco, beginning in the year 1954. Leaving their old homes in Casablanca, Meknes, or B'Nimilal, the immigrants were swept into a vast colonizing scheme. After arrival in Israel, they were quickly dispatched to Oren. They had never dreamed the dream of "conquering the desert," nor did they desire to become part of a new generation of Jewish farmers. They were ill prepared for their new role and understood little of the plans and ideals that were shaping their lives. These immigrants (and others like them) did not wish to become "pioneers," but in effect they acted that role. Paradoxically, they fulfilled an ideal they did not create and precisely at a time when those who first conceived the ideal were responding less actively to its demands.

Both "pioneering" and "reluctance" are important aspects of Israeli immigrant villages. Important as they are, however, they express only part of the immigrants' situation. Consider this swift turn of events: when the immigrants arrived at Oren in 1954, none of them had any experience in farming, and none had ever before lived in a cooperative community. Israeli village conditions were new and wholly different from their Moroccan experience. The years that followed were, as might be expected, rife with interpersonal tensions and group conflicts. And yet, unexpectedly perhaps, six years later all the settlers were working as farmers, and some had prospered; and the village had begun to be a viable community. Their reluctance was tempered by social and material rewards, and they had begun to sink roots in the village. Explaining how and why these changes took place is the major aim of this study.

The problem is to understand "change," yet, as in all such cases, the circumstances of Oren's development are somewhat special. The settlers were immigrants, they had never farmed before, and they were Jews immigrating to a Jewish State. These are all distinctive factors that figure prominently in the analysis. Further, Oren is representative of an "administered community"—a community whose social, cultural, economic, and political development is directed by outside agencies—and these special conditions influenced the village's growth. Planning, external control, and paternalism characterize this type of community. The directing group, the Jewish Agency's Settlement Department, planned and financed the village's physical development and guided the immigrants' introduction to farming and village life. Instructors assigned to the village managed community economic and political affairs and also sought to introduce changes in the immigrants' cultural traditions. Changes were initiated from outside the community, and although the villagers did not lack power themselves, they were dependent rather than autonomous.

Studying Oren's development therefore means analyzing the ways in which government planning and administrative activities influenced the village. The problem may be stated as follows: given the conditions of bureaucratically directed villages, how do administrative policies affect a community's growth? Variations in policy can be seen to mark off periods in the village's development; changes introduced in the village's form of organization underlie stages in its growth. Thus, in the first period, from 1954 to 1955, the village was organized as a plantation: land was not parceled out to the settlers, but rather the settlers worked as wage laborers under the direction of Department-appointed managers. During this initial stage, a village committee was elected, but the managers dominated the decision-making process. In the second period, from 1955 to 1960, the Department allocated individual plots of land to each settler, and the village began to function as a typical producers' cooperative. Although most settlers began to farm, many soon became discouraged, since they found farming difficult and unrewarding. The village credit system was tightly centralized so that settler cooperation and interdependence were emphasized. During this period the settlers became more actively involved in formulating village policies, but the Department managers continued to hold crucial administrative and political positions. Village factionalism, based mainly upon opposed clusters of kinsmen, flourished, and the recurrent factional disputes often threatened to disrupt community life entirely.

The middle portion of this study—Chapters IV, V, and VI—concentrates upon this second period in Oren's development. The final chapter analyzes the turn of events that distinguish the third period. In this latter phase, from 1960 to 1962, the Department initiated a new, individualistic credit system, and economic interdependence among the settlers began to diminish. This reform resulted in a muting of factional strife and an intensification of agricultural activity. More experienced in farming, some settlers mastered the farming techniques and even began to prosper. At the same time, the village became more autonomous as village direction was transferred to the settlers themselves. Thus, in brief, the three periods between 1954 and 1962 are distinguished by changes in administrative policy as the villagers, responding to changing circumstances, learned to adjust to farming and village life.

This résumé has placed particular emphasis upon the administered nature of the community. The conditions mentioned characterize all of the 280 immigrant villages formed since 1948, and in this regard Oren represents a larger class of Israeli communities. While their external conditions are similar, however, not all of these newly created villages have followed Oren's course of development. In some villages comparatively few settlers have become farmers; in others, factional disputes continue to disrupt community affairs; and in still others, apathy or disorganization characterizes the social fabric. If the external conditions are similar, what accounts for these variations in social and political development? Aspects of internal social organization— in particular, the villagers' social origins, primary group networks, and factional alignments—mainly explain the variations. In other words, the same policy introduced into two different communities will have different consequences, depending upon the village's social and political structure. Part of this study— especially the final chapter—is devoted to a comparative review of how these factors affect village growth. Administered village development is influenced by both sets of variables: by the plans proposed and implemented, and by the internal shape of the community.

Although brief and still in flux, the Israeli experience raises many general problems in directed change. What is involved in the transition from dependent to autonomous communities? How does a "traditional" social system become "modern"? Is rapid change possible, and, if so, what factors determine the extent and rate of change? While the referent throughout is the Israeli situation, the problems and processes described in this study may be relevant to other times and places. Administered village schemes have recently been introduced in other countries, and the Israeli experience points out factors important in the growth of communities of this type.

Directed change is one theme of this study. A major complementary theme is an analysis of culture contact. Emigration to Israel and settlement at Oren brought Moroccans into close contact with members of the veteran Israeli community. As might be expected, the new relationships produced important changes in the immigrants' lives. In addition, they led to changes within the veteran population. The mutual effects of contact have not always been sufficiently appreciated in studies of culture change. This process of reciprocal change—the varieties of ways in which all groups in contact become altered—is described in Chapter VII. The types of change differ for each group, but they are far-reaching for both.

It may be of interest, as part of this introduction, to consider briefly how the material analyzed in the study was gathered. Fortunately, and also necessarily, it came from two different vantage points: from within the village and from within the development authority. The study was begun in December, 1957. I lived at Oren (part of the time with my family) until the following October. From then until June, 1959, I visited regularly in the village and collected comparative material in several other Moroccan communities. The data were gathered by means of the now traditional anthropological techniques: formal interviews with nearly all of the settlers, much more intensive interviews with a smaller number of informants, and, most important, participation in the daily life of the village. This part of my research was made possible by a grant from the Ford Foundation, and I wish to thank the officers of the Foundation for their generous support.

Following this research, I continued to study immigrant villages but in a different capacity. Beginning in 1959 and continuing until 1962, I was appointed Director of Social Research in the Jewish Agency Settlement Department. The purpose of this project was to develop a program of applied social research in the Department. With my Israeli colleagues, I continued the studies begun earlier and participated in studies of other villages. This experience within the development authority provided a different perspective of the settlement system. Whereas previously I had "looked up" to the Department from the vantage point of the village, I could later consider the village from the perspective of the Department's planners and administrators. Both perspectives were necessary. This twin vision enabled me to see more clearly how the interests of the different groups might clash, merge, or become adjusted to one another.

It was, to be sure, a remarkably enlightening experience, and I am indebted to many persons who assisted me generously during this research. My friends at Oren encouraged me to learn about their community and helped me to understand their lives in the new situation. The officers of the Settlement Department were also gracious and cooperative at all times. I wish in particular to thank Mr. Michah Talmon, the former Director of the Negev Authority, and Dr. Raanan Weitz, Chairman of the Settlement Department, for their friendship and assistance. In addition, I benefited greatly from the experience and wise counsel of my colleagues on the Department's social research staff: Rivka

Rehat, Nomi Navo, Zippora Stup, Ovadya Shapiro, Moshe Minkovitz, and Shlomo Deshen.

I am further indebted to my teachers and colleagues, who helped me to formulate the problems described in this study. Professors Sol Tax, Fred Eggan, Clifford Geertz, Elihu Katz, Leonard Binder, and Morris Janowitz, of the University of Chicago, S. N. Eisenstadt, of the Hebrew University, Arnold Strickon and David Kaplan, of Brandeis University, and Max Gluckman, of the University of Manchester, commented critically on various drafts of this manuscript. I wish to thank each of them for their encouragement and help. Brandeis University provided a generous grant for preparing the manuscript, and I would like to thank the University for its support. Finally, the kind assistance of Menucha Peleg, who provided a working place, Betty Griffin, who edited and typed the manuscript, and Ilsa Schuster, who prepared the index, is gratefully acknowledged.

Earlier versions of portions of this study appeared in the following journals: *Middle East Journal*, XIV (1960); *Economic Development and Cultural Change*, XI (1962); and *American Anthropologist*, LXIV (1962). I would like to thank the editors and publishers of these journals for permission to reprint this material.

A. W.

Waltham, Massachusetts
September 1965

Contents

RELUCTANT PIONEERS
Village Development in Israel

CHAPTER I

Historical Perspective: Morocco and Israel

TWO different cultural traditions are represented in Israeli immigrant villages: the traditions of the immigrant groups and
those of the veteran Israeli population. The immigrants in this
study are Moroccan Jews—more specifically, those Moroccan
immigrants who settled in a new farming community. Although
numerically a small group, these immigrants reflect many features characteristic of Moroccan Jewish culture. On the other
hand, the traditions they confronted in Israel are European in
origin, and they are most directly expressed through the government agencies engaged in immigrant agricultural settlement.

This situation defines a classic case of "culture contact": the
Moroccan immigrants and the Israeli officials were placed in
contact within the context of a small community. The bearers of
two different ways of life met, interacted, and influenced one
another. A village's growth was continually influenced by this
interplay of traditions. Indeed, to understand the development
of a village, one must first study the traditions of the two
groups. How and why immigrant villages took the course they

did is clarified by examining the cultural traditions of the groups in contact.

Such an examination of the two cultures is the main purpose of this chapter. However, it is a selective examination; a complete analysis of both cultures is beyond the scope of this study. Here, the analysis focuses upon those social processes and cultural ideals which have a special relevance for the formation and development of an immigrant village.

*The Immigrants: Moroccan Jewish
Society and Culture*

Although many of the details are still lacking, Jewry's lineage in Morocco is old and probably ancient. The contemporary Moroccan Jewish community can be traced to three groups: the original Palestinian *émigrés*, inland Berber groups, and Jews who migrated from Spain to Morocco. Moroccan Jewish history is, at least in part, the study of how these three groups settled in the country, and how they adapted to one another and to their neighbors.

Briefly described, Jewish settlement in Morocco may date from as early as the third or second century B.C. The first settlers were probably immigrants from Palestine and other Middle Eastern countries (mainly Egypt and Cyrenaica) who came to the Maghreb in search of political refuge and economic well-being.[1] The Roman conquest of North Africa (Carthage fell in 146 B.C.) and Rome's subsequent rule led to additional Jewish colonization. By the end of the third century A.D., flourishing colonies of Jewish merchants and artisans were formed throughout Roman Africa. These groups were small in size, and they tended to cluster within the more secure coastal towns. While politically dependent upon their Roman masters, Jews were

[1] A good over-all survey of Moroccan Jewish history is contained in A. Chouraqui, *Les Juifs d'Afrique du Nord: Marche vers l'Occident* (Paris: Presses Universitaires de France, 1952). Throughout the present study, "Middle East" is used in its larger sense to include North Africa.

nonetheless permitted to develop an autonomous social and cultural life. They maintained close contact with Palestine and, later, Babylonia, and thereby retained ties with the major Jewish cultural centers.

While Jewish-Roman relations in Africa were typically cordial, the rise of Christianity during the fourth century produced a series of crises between Jews and Roman Christians, particularly over the question of proselytization. Jews were active missionaries to the Berbers, apparently meeting with some success. Proselytization perhaps accounts for the so-called "Berber-Jews": Jewish groups appear in the inland Berber regions, and their origin may be traced partially to conversions.[2]

Rome's dominion spelled relative peace and prosperity. The fifth-century Vandal invasions, however, brought widespread destruction and unrest, and in the ensuing pillage some Jews fled to the interior. The later establishment of Byzantine rule (533) resulted in a general pacification, although it was also marked by intermittent anti-Jewish policies. The political climate was comparatively favorable, however, and when Spanish Jews were expelled from that land in 613 and again in 681, many found refuge in neighboring Morocco. There they formed sociocultural enclaves within the Jewish town quarters. This immigration of Spanish Jews (repeated again on a much larger scale in 1131 and 1491) introduced the third element in the Moroccan Jewish population. Although forming a single political community, each of these three groups maintained its own distinctive customs—so much so, in fact, that until recent times intermarriage between them was limited.[3]

[2] There seems to be some evidence of conversion of Berbers to Judaism. For example, the early Church fathers complained of the missionary activities of the Jews. At the same time, however, Jewish migration into the inland Berber areas took place. It is therefore difficult to determine whether the Jewish population in Berber regions stems from conversion or more simply from migration. Both factors were no doubt important.

[3] See R. Le Tourneau, *Fes avant le Protectorat* (Casablanca: SMLE Société Marocaine, 1949), p. 184.

North Africa's cultural future was cast, however, from the East and not the West: by the year 713 Arab conquerors had swept to the Atlantic, and Islam's rule was indelibly fixed upon the Maghreb. Islam's dominion had an enormous impact upon Moroccan Jewry—Jewish life was deeply influenced by centuries of close contact with Moroccan Muslim civilization. Taken as a whole, Moroccan Jewry in the period between the eighth and the early twentieth century may be thought of as a "traditional community." Certainly this is a simplification—Muslim-Jewish relations differed between regions and also varied according to the outlook of particular ruling dynasties—and yet there is a core of social, political, and cultural tradition that distinguishes Jewry throughout this period.

In Morocco, as throughout Islam, Jews held the status of *dhimmi*, protected peoples.[4] The *dhimmi* contract defined the Jews' "duties towards Muslims," as well as the temporal rights they were to receive.[5] A Jew's duties included paying regular taxes (*djezya*) and special levies to the state. They also were required to "submit to certain humiliating conditions with regard to dress, housing and possessions, intending to distinguish them from Muslims."[6] For example, males wore a black robe, or *jellaba*, and Jews lived in segregated quarters. Furthermore, they were barred from citizenship in the state and had to assume a "general respectful attitude towards Muslims."[7] As is apparent in these restrictions, Jews were both legally and socially subordinate to the Muslim community. Tolerance was often expressed, but misery and humiliation were more typically the Jews' lot.

Although it placed the Jews in a subordinate position, the

[4] For a general discussion of the *dhimmi* status, see M. Th. Houtsma, et al., *The Encyclopedia of Islam* (Leyden: Brill, 1913–1936), p. 331.

[5] *Ibid.*, p. 331.

[6] R. Levy, *The Social Structure of Islam* (Cambridge: University Press, 1957), p. 254.

[7] Houtsma, *op. cit.*, p. 331.

dhimmi status guaranteed their life and property, and allocated internal control to Jewish authorities. The political framework was typically feudal: the Sultan or local *cheikh* was responsible for protecting "his Jews"; in exchange for defense he collected heavy taxes and freely called upon the special skills of Jewish craftsmen. Internal communal affairs were administered by Jewish officials: rabbinic courts settled disputes between Jews, community councils were responsible for taxation and charity, and the Jewish *cheikh* represented the *dhimmi* before the Muslim authorities.

This system—like the general Moroccan structure of authority—was obviously fragile: so long as peace reigned and the central authorities maintained effective control, it functioned smoothly. However, peace has been the exception in Moroccan history, and intrigue and revolt the rule. Instability, whether caused by prolonged drought or the death of the Sultan, exposed the Jews to grave dangers; violence and persecution could break out at any time. Historically, the Jews' dependent political position resulted in moments of peace and prosperity, regularly punctuated by riot and ruin.

Throughout Morocco the area of prescribed Jewish residence was called the *millah*. The *millah* was either a walled quarter within a town (as in Fez and Merrakech) or a small village adjoining rural Arab or Berber villages. The traditional *millah* of Fez, for example, is described as "being boxed into a limited area," and was "forced to attain in height and density that which it lacked in area. As a consequence the buildings were high, typically of two stories. . . . The higher part of the *millah* constituted the aristocratic quarter; here one finds spacious homes. . . . The lower quarter, much more miserable, dense and hot, sheltered the humbler classes and the small workshops where the Jewish artisans worked." [8] In the best of circumstances the *millah* was congested and lacked adequate sanitary facilities.

[8] Le Tourneau, *op. cit.*, pp. 102–104.

Many Jews were employed as tradesmen and artisans—
peddlers, smiths, tailors, or petty merchants.[9] Some were engaged in work ritually barred to Muslims; for example, work in
precious metals, moneylending, and the sale of intoxicants were
Jewish monopolies. However, they were forbidden to purchase
land and thereby were barred from farming. Certain other skills
(masonry, for example) were also dominated by Muslims. This
division of labor led to a type of intergroup economic cooperation: specialization tied the groups to one another and
tended to reduce competition between Jews and Muslims.

Viewed from within, the *millah* was dominated by an elite
group composed of religious specialists and wealthy families. Between the ninth and thirteenth centuries, and for a brief period
following the immigration of Spanish Jews in 1491, Morocco
was an important center of Jewish learning. For example, the
academies of Fez and Merrakech contributed respected commentaries on law. When in later centuries these intellectual traditions waned, religious custom and ritual continued to guide
behavior: the Jewish communities were orthodox in religious
expression, and the Bible and commentaries formed a manual to
daily life. The various sacred specialists—rabbi, religious judge,
or ritual functionary—were part of the *millah* elite. The rabbis
guarded traditional attitudes, and deviant behavior was severely
punished. The learned, pious rabbis were models of morality,
and they were also seated in formal community councils.

Wealth, too, lent influence: the wealthy merchants and finan-
ciers (always a tiny fraction of the population) were powerful
figures, and they were counted among the elite. The most
affluent were the few "court Jews" who catered to the Sultan
and who, in return, received spectacular benefits. In general, social status depended upon learning, wealth, and family ties; distinguished rabbis and heads of wealthy families held the key

[9] For a more detailed listing of Jewish occupations see J. Goulven,
Les Mellahs de Rabat-Sale (Paris: Editions Larose, 1923).

posts. Although social mobility was possible, there was a dynastic slant to the *millah:* the influential families tended to dominate each community.

Social relations within the *millah* hinged upon family and kinship ties. While a man might legally take more than one wife, the number of polygamous marriages was limited. Residence tended to be patrilocal, although a newly married couple might live with the wife's parents if her family was wealthy. Typically, marriages were arranged and tended to take place at an early age: the bride might be ten or twelve, the groom only slightly older.[10] Marriage between kinsmen was preferred and seems to have taken place frequently.

Male and female roles within the family unit were clearly defined. Males were dominant: men worked in the craft stalls or market, prayed in the synagogue, and meted out punishment when necessary. Women were subservient to their husband's wishes: they had "an almost completely domestic role," and a wife "did not overtly disagree with her husband's opinions or decisions." [11] Men received at least an elementary religious instruction while few females were formally educated.

Family units were, in turn, joined into larger patrilineal extended groups. The extended family was composed of a man and his wife or wives, married sons and their families, and unmarried sons and daughters. This group undertook important cooperative activities. The linked families maintained a joint household: each family lived in its own room, but meals were eaten in a common kitchen. In addition, the male family members often worked together, and the females were jointly responsible for keeping house. The junior family members were directed in these tasks by the elder parents: the patriarch guided occupa-

[10] See Elie Malka, *Essai d'Ethnographie des Mellahs* (Rabat: Imprerie Omnia, 1946), p. 54.

[11] M. Jacobs, *A Study of Culture Stability and Change: The Moroccan Jewess* (Washington: Catholic University Press, 1956), p. 19.

tional activities, and the elder mother supervised the household
chores. The patriarch also controlled the joint purse; for example, a married son who wished to make a major purchase first
consulted his father. Generally speaking, the eldest son was the
most influential among the brothers. Although daughters left
home at marriage, they too continued to maintain close ties with
their parents.

With age and time, family leadership was transferred from father to sons, who then became responsible for their aging parents. This transition was often tense, as parents and children
shifted uneasily into a new pattern of relationships. Following
the death of the patriarch, the sons inherited equal shares, with
the exception of the eldest son, who received a double share.[12]
Depending upon the circumstances, brothers either continued to
cooperate or split into separate units, ultimately to become new
extended families.

Another important social group was based upon kinship. Although the boundaries of kinship were fluid, this group was bi-
lateral in form, including both sets of maternal and paternal
grandparents, their siblings and descendants, as well as maternal
and paternal uncles and aunts and their children. Kinsmen visited
one another on family fetes, sometimes cooperated in economic
ventures, and joined forces in moments of crisis or conflict. Although both maternal and paternal links were recognized, the
patrilineal kinsmen had special functions. For example, patrilineal kinsmen often prayed together in the synagogue and joined
in other devotional groups. The male of highest status within

---

[12] Two different systems of inheritance were practiced: the Castilian
and what Jacobs calls the Mosaic, or Biblical. Under the former the
widow receives half of the inheritance, and the other half is divided
between siblings regardless of sex (with the exception of the eldest son,
who receives a double share). Under the Mosaic system the widow receives an amount equal to her dowry, unmarried daughters receive a
tenth share, and the sons divide the remainder, the eldest son receiving
a double portion.

this group was recognized as its informal leader and was turned to for guidance and consultation.

Each *millah* comprised a tightly knit, intimate community. Jews as a group stood apart from their Muslim neighbors—the lines of communal cleavage were distinct. Social relations between Jews and Muslims were typically formal and circumscribed. Intermarriage rarely occurred. Cultural interchanges, however, were many and continuous. Jews spoke an Arabic dialect in the *millah* and Arabic or Berber with Muslims. They shared with the Muslims their beliefs in the healing powers of saints, the evil eye, the value of potions, or the fear of devils. Both Muslims and Jews made religious pilgrimages to the same sites.[13] Even though the more rationalistic rule of the rabbis was maintained, these layers of common folk belief were deeply rooted in the *millah*.

Fragmented between warring Berber tribes and an inept central government, Morocco suffered a deep politico-economic decline in the period between the sixteenth and the twentieth centuries. The ruinous conditions had a disastrous effect upon the Jewish communities.[14] Outbreaks of anti-Jewish violence were common, and the traditional restrictions were pressed to their limit. This political instability and economic depression resulted in an increasingly pauperized Jewry. Although the rabbis' rule remained firm, the old traditions of learning began to wither. Indeed, Moroccan Jewry gradually fell away from the mainstream of Jewish historical development and became increasingly isolated and peripheral. Thus, to sum up briefly, at the turn of the twentieth century Morocco's Jews retained their traditional dependent contract with the Muslim population; Jews were primarily artisans and peddlers; the extended family and kin groups

[13] The pilgrimage tradition is excellently documented in L. Voinot, *Pelerinages Judeo-Musulmans du Maroc* (Paris: Larose, 1949).

[14] For example, see A. Sarfaty, "Yahas Fes," *Hesperis,* XIX (1934); and G. Vajda, "Un Recueil de Textes Historiques Judeo Marocains," *Hesperis,* XXXV (1948), and XXXVI (1949).

were important social units; and the rabbis and the rich dominated a *millah* firmly devoted to religious ritual.

This "traditional community" began to change rapidly when
in 1912 French troops occupied Morocco and established the
Protectorate (the French took control of Algeria in 1830, and of
Tunisia in 1871). Contact with Europe had long been maintained by a handful of wealthy merchants in the coastal towns,
but the French occupation had an immediate, revolutionary
effect upon the entire Jewish community.

French idealism as represented by General Lyautey, the first
Resident-General, dreamed of a Morocco transformed, a modern land that would still retain the beauty of the old and traditional. French administrators sought not to disturb tradition, but
to encircle it gently with modern Europe. For example, rather
than jar a "jeweled Fez," Lyautey built a modern French quarter outside the old walls; Casablanca, a sleepy fishing village in
1900, became the "second Paris." Taxation, community organization and administration, and the legal system were all reorganized under the direction of French officials. New school systems
were built, and French was spoken in the streets as well as in the
schools. Moreover, after great effort the French Army finally
succeeded in achieving what the Sultans had failed to accomplish
in five hundred years: the Berber tribes were pacified, and Morocco began to be a single nation. Relative peace and security
reigned in the land.

Lyautey saw wisdom in conservatism: the French were to
administer Muslim tradition, though curbing the dangerous or
obnoxious. In keeping with this approach, the Jews, who had
been *dhimmi* and not citizens of the Muslim state, remained in a
special class of noncitizens: the state was no longer theocratic,
but it was Muslim, and the Jews became "Moroccan-Jews"
rather than "Moroccans." Similarly, the French retained the
Jewish internal political system: rabbinic courts maintained their
jurisdiction, local *millah* councils were formalized, and a national

Jewish board was formed. On the other hand, in a series of decrees the French abolished many of the old Jewish restrictions: Jews might henceforth live where they pleased, dress as they chose, and go where they liked; the old capricious tax system was rescinded; moreover, life and property was guaranteed by the force of French arms. Thus, although their political emancipation was only partial, the Jews' daily lot was vastly improved.[15]

The Protectorate also opened up new economic possibilities. While most Jews continued to follow their traditional occupations, a minority entered into new crafts and industries.[16] To some degree this brought Jews and Muslims into competition, since members of both groups sought the same new positions. Along with these developments, and perhaps most significant of all, the Protectorate introduced secular, European culture to Morocco. A new cultural model was present—the modern Frenchman—and its influence was soon pervasive. Some Jews were earlier prepared for this: in 1863 the Alliance Israélite Universelle began providing small numbers of Jewish students with a secular French education. The Protectorate now generalized this tendency: European attitudes became fashionable, secular tendencies developed, and behavior patterns began shifting.

As may be readily imagined, the Jews responded enthusiastically to this transformation; they gladly exchanged their former servile position for a new dependence upon the French. Since French control was greatest in the major cities, the Jews (as well as many Muslims) flocked to the new French towns. Migration to Casablanca was especially contagious: French Casablanca, which did not exist in 1912, included nearly 40 per cent of the total Jewish population of Morocco in 1947.[17] Although in the-

---

[15] For a general description of these changes, see A. Weingrod, "Moroccan Jewry in Transition" (in Hebrew), *Megamot*, IX, No. 3 (1960).

[16] See Chouraqui, *op. cit.*, pp. 358–359.   [17] *Ibid.*, p. 340.

ory the Jews might live where they pleased, they generally tended to congregate in a new or old *millah*. Always crammed, the Jewish quarters soon became incredibly crowded: to cite an extreme case, population density in the *millah* of Meknes reached the rate of 400,000 per square mile! [18] As population density rose, the *millah* took on the characteristics of an urban slum. "It seems incredible," Chouraqui writes, "that an entire population was squeezed into a narrow area, without gardens, water, sunlight or air." [19] Effective social controls were undermined by these conditions: the rising statistics of crime and delinquency attest to the crises brought on by urban slum life. Moreover, these various factors combined to produce a splintering of the community. The wealthy families and the more secular youngsters tended to flee from the crowded *millah* and take up residence in the new French quarters, while the poor, the old, and the more traditional families remained.

Although French values represented the direction of change, acculturation was generally limited to the wealthy and the school-trained youngsters. Jacobs writes that "the wealthy elite . . . was at the forefront of acculturation," while the *millah* masses "belong to the Middle Ages." [20] Even though the wealthy families may have expressed "a certain ambivalence towards the values and conditions of the modern world," class and acculturation were positively correlated.[21] For the broad mass of *millah* poor—the majority by far—the old norms and values remained strong: in the *millah*'s twisting alleys the old traditions were maintained. Migration, urbanization, and cultural differentiation were thus the dominant features of the post-1912 period.

These changes led further to a reorganization of social relations. Migration and city life weakened the old family and kin-

---

[18] *Ibid.*, p. 167.   [19] *Ibid.*, p. 183.

[20] Jacobs, *op. cit.*, p. 52; and I. Abbou, *Musulmans, Andalous, et Judeo Espagnols* (Casablanca: Editions Antar, 1953), p. 429.

[21] Jacobs, *op. cit.*, p. 57.

ship ties. Marriages were increasingly based upon personal choice rather than family arrangement, and a trend toward neo-local residence grew. Similarly, traditional patterns of patriarchal control and sibling unity came under growing pressure. Young men were successfully able to challenge their father's authority: young people in rural regions left for the city, where they established separate households. Cooperative economic activities became less frequent. The rapid migration broke the unity of the kinship group, since kinsmen were now scattered in different towns and cities. At the same time, kinship sometimes tended to assume new definitions: migrants who shared common descent searched each other out, so that certain types of relationships, never before powerful, became effective.

The period of the Protectorate was characterized by change and crisis—and new opportunities. Of course, the Muslim community was also affected by these developments. However, unlike the Jews, the Muslims experienced a growing anti-colonial nationalist feeling. Particularly following the close of the Second World War, the demand for Moroccan independence became insistent. For the Jews, Moroccan nationalism was something of an anomaly: Jews had never seriously considered themselves to be "Moroccans" (a status from which they were, of course, barred). They were Jews in a Muslim-Jewish system that had recently become a Muslim-Jewish-French system. Although a few did participate in the nationalist movement, for the vast majority the thought of Morocco without the French was a nightmare.[22] Might the Jews conceivably depend upon the good graces of the Arabs and Berbers? Could they become truly integrated within a sovereign Morocco? As the nationalist cry grew and terrorism spread, the Jewish community grew increasingly apprehensive over its future.

Events soon reached a climax, but in a totally unanticipated

[22] For a general discussion of this problem, see H. Lehrman, "Morocco's Jews between Israel and France," *Commentary*, XX (1955), 393–402.

fashion. Like other Jewish Diaspora communities, Moroccan Jewry had long maintained traditional ties with Palestine. For example, the collection of moneys for Palestinian charities was an old custom. During the 1930's a small Moroccan Zionist organization was established, and throughout the twentieth century a trickle of immigrants left for Palestine. Political developments during the middle and late 1940's—the possibility of a Jewish State in Palestine—suddenly brought the Zionist issue into greater prominence. Zionist emissaries initiated small-scale educational and propaganda work in Morocco. Then, in 1948 Israel was established, and war broke out between Israel and the neighboring Arab countries. The immediate effect of this conflict was a deterioration of Muslim-Jewish relations in Morocco and even greater uncertainty regarding the future. A series of anti-Jewish massacres took place during the summer of 1948.[23] Fear swept the Jewish communities. At the same time, Israel, now a political reality, opened its doors and actively encouraged immigration. Many Jews began to consider emigration to Israel as the only possible solution to their dilemma. Their fate in Morocco was in doubt; Israel appealed for immigrants; moreover, they would be immigrants in a Jewish State, in the Holy Land! Thus, beginning in 1948 and with mounting tempo, tens of thousands of Moroccan Jews began emigrating to Israel.

The Receiving Society: Cultural Foundations

This analysis has thus far examined some aspects of Moroccan Jewry. In the pages that follow we will be concerned with the receiving society, the Israelis.

Here too, the presentation is selective and stresses some of the groups within the Jewish community while neglecting others. The emphasis is upon the "pioneer immigrants," particularly those who founded new agricultural settlements. This partiality does not mean that all or even many of the pre-1948 Jewish set-

[23] See Chouraqui, *op. cit.*, pp. 125–126.

tlers were pioneers: some were refugees, others lived in closed religious enclaves, and still others were engaged in middle-class business activities. Although they were a minority, the pioneer groups provided political leadership in the Jewish community, and thereby they were able to infuse their viewpoints throughout the society. The following analysis therefore concentrates upon them.

Jewish Israel is almost entirely an immigrant community. While small numbers of Jews lived there for centuries, the dominant features of the Jewish society were formed by recent groups of immigrants. Outstanding among these are Eastern European Jews: as Isaiah Berlin points out, "the Jews of Russia and Poland . . . are most closely concerned with the early foundations of Israel." [24] These Eastern European immigrants, who first came to Palestine near the close of the nineteenth century, led the formation of the modern Jewish State. To understand this immigrant group is to comprehend the cultural basis of Israeli society.

These immigrants must first be seen in the light of their time —in the perspective of a unique cultural situation. They were part of a generation in revolt: revolt against Jewish statelessness (the "Jewish condition"), against the rule of religious orthodoxy, and what is more, against the existing social order. Just as nineteenth-century Russian intelligentsia seethed with new ideas and countless intrigues, so too did Eastern European Jewish intellectual groups. It was an age of movements and ideals, and the Jews "assimilated the humanist-liberal, radical, and social-democratic traditions of intellectual revolt which the best elements of these countries developed." [25] Within the revolutionary tide flowed the idea of Zionism—the establishment of a Jewish State in Palestine. Zionist programs were debated, mani-

[24] I. Berlin, "The Origins of Israel," in *The Middle East in Transition,* ed. by W. Laquer (London: Routledge and Kegan Paul, 1958), p. 208.
[25] *Ibid.,* p. 210.

festos issued, and parties formed. Then some—very few indeed
—took the dramatic step and emigrated to Palestine.[26] They
were mainly young, unmarried males, most of whom had been
"students from secondary schools, Universities and Theological
seminaries, laborers, skilled artisans, officials, teachers, writers
and other professionals." [27]

The immigrants' ideology—the vision that drew them—is
well illustrated in the following passage; these brief sentences
epitomize the revolutionary program.

The terrible position of the Jewish nation will not be improved unless
we emigrate, alter our ways of life, and engage in productive work.
Every nation lives on a land of its own; the majority of its members
are farmers living by the toil of their hands, the rest being engaged
in other branches of work that have visible results and are of real
value. The Jewish people have become a people of "the spirit,"
logicians, merchants, and middlemen; and for this reason it has become physically improvised. . . . Let us therefore summon our
strength and start out. Let us return to our ancient Mother, to the
country which awaits us full of compassion, to nourish us with the
best of her fruit. Let us abandon the scale and measure and take up
the plough and sickle.[28]

Zionism, socialism, and pioneering were the primary ideals
expressed in this social movement. Zionism demanded immigration to Palestine; immigration alone would solve the "terrible
position of the Jewish nation" by placing it upon "a land of its
own." In addition, Zionism emphasized the creation of political
and economic conditions that would permit the formation of a

[26] According to estimates, from 1882 to 1914 between 55,000 and 70,000
Jews immigrated to Palestine. In the period between 1919 and 1947
Jewish immigration totaled 444,833. These figures are taken from the
Statistical Abstract of Israel, No. 9, p. 59.

[27] S. Dayan, *Moshav Ovdim* (Tel Aviv: Palestine Pioneer Library No.
6, 1947), p. 6.

[28] I. L. Pinsker, quoted in D. Ben Gurion, *Jewish Labour* (London:
Hechalutz Organization of England, 1936), p. 3.

total Jewish community. The immigrants conceived of themselves as the vanguard of a future, much larger immigration wave: they were "to pave the road for the return of the masses of Jews to their land." [29]

The immigrants' socialism was a many-faceted concept. In the first place, socialism meant the establishment of a new, nonexploitative economic order; the newcomers' intellectual heritage stressed the ideal of classlessness. Then, too, socialism provided for a society emphasizing cooperation and controlled by democratic community planning. Indeed, planning was a hallmark of the movement: rational techniques would promote the construction of a revolutionary social system. When coupled with pioneering, socialism also meant an almost mystical attempt at personal transformation: it spelled a turn to physical labor, abandoning "the scale and measure" and taking up "the plow and sickle." A Jewish, nonexploitative state could not be built upon Arab labor: Jews must "conquer labor" and become workers. Young intellectuals turned to work "in the quarries, as stone-masons, digging ditches, boring walls, handling and carrying goods." [30] In this fashion it was not only society which was being transformed, it was also man: the "logician" turned laborer was altering his very self.

Pioneering was the purest distillation of the immigrants' dreams. A pioneer (*chalutz*) dedicated himself to achieving the goals of Socialist-Zionism. Pioneering was mainly associated with agricultural settlements: pioneers were those who left the settled towns and established farming communities in remote, barren areas. This "elite within an elite" strove to realize national, socialist, and personal goals: they were settling the land of a nation-to-be, building a new social order, and also, by this very process, transforming themselves. The *chalutz* was therefore the first among equals.

The *kibbutz* and *moshav*, classic types of Jewish farming set-

[29] *Ibid.*, p. 7.   [30] *Ibid.*, p. 18.

tlements, illustrate many of the ideals of the new culture.[31] The
kibbutz is a communal agricultural village in which the primary
social unit is the commune, or adult membership.[32] Work in the
kibbutz is collectively organized, and economic gain or loss is
shared by the members according to democratic decision: no
wages are paid, but the collective provides for each member's
wants. The community is, ideally, classless. Moreover, both men
and women work, and children are cared for in special quarters;
they do not live with their parents, and as a consequence, the
family is stripped of its usual economic and socializing functions.
Within this framework the *kibbutz* seeks to realize the values of
self-labor and colonization, cooperation and democracy, nonex-
ploitation and community planning. The *kibbutz* has traditionally represented the epitome of pioneering and symbolized the
elite goals.

Since the development of a Moroccan *moshav* is the primary
topic of this study, it is important to consider the *moshav* system
in greater detail. Like the *kibbutz*, the *moshav*'s organizational
principles grew out of the East European immigrants' desire to
create the "good society." In contrast with the *kibbutz*, however, the founders of the *moshav* wished to preserve the family
unit. In this regard, the *moshav* was a reaction to the *kibbutz*'s
extreme communalism: the latter was criticized for depriving
"the settlers of the joys of normal family life" and also because
"it did not permit the exercise of initiative and free play of abili-

[31] A third type of community, the *moshava*, originated in the Baron
de Rothschild's colonization schemes of the late nineteenth century. These
communities were based upon vineyards or citriculture. Private forms
of ownership and work were practiced, and laborers were usually recruited from among the local Muslim population. These settlements—for
example, Rechovot, Zichron Yaacov and Rishon L'Zion—have since
grown into small towns.

[32] A recent analysis of the *kibbutz* is contained in M. Spiro, *Kibbutz:
Venture in Utopia* (Cambridge: Harvard University Press, 1956). For
an "inside view" of *kibbutz* life, see M. Weingarten, *Life in a Kibbutz*
(New York: Reconstructionist Press, 1955).

ties of the great majority of the settlers." [33] As expressed in the *moshav*, the "good society" meant the merger of family-based individualism with community-wide cooperation.

The *moshav* is, in essence, a cooperative farming village. The family is the basic socioeconomic unit: every family lives in its own home and works its land according to its own abilities and desires. Moreover, individual initiative is an integral part of the system; the successful farmer benefits directly from his labor. Indeed, personal initiative and achievement are highly prized.

The *moshav*'s organizing principles also express the founders' more idealistic hopes: self-labor, equality of opportunity, mutual aid, cooperation, and community democracy are key elements of the *moshav* system. Self-labor has, as Dayan correctly notes, a "dual implication." "One is that the settler and his family shall work their land themselves, the other that no outside labor may be employed." [34] Emphasizing the settlers' own labor is in consonance with the stress placed upon physical work. Moreover, by stressing the positive value of labor, exploitation is ruled out: since work is in itself good, it naturally follows that the hiring of outside labor is prohibited. In this fashion the *moshav* is to be a community of workers and *ipso facto*, a classless society.

Equality of opportunity is another *moshav* principle. "The Moshav aims at the maximum of economic equality among its members, and does everything in its power to assure such equality. . . . All the holdings are of equal size. . . . Loans for equipment, buildings and livestock are of equal amounts for all the holdings. Equality of opportunity is thus assured for every settler." [35] This equal distribution of resources—land, water, and loans—further strengthens the ideal of classlessness.[36] However, equal opportunities never means identical incomes: what is important is that every member has an equal chance, not that each will receive identical rewards.

[33] Dayan, *op. cit.*, pp. 17–18.   [34] *Ibid.*, pp. 22–23.
[35] *Ibid.*, p. 26.   [36] *Ibid.*

Equality of opportunity permits difference: since there are "differences in physical capacity, skill, power of judgement, initiative and executive ability as between one settler and another," it is obvious that some will prosper more than others.[37] Mutual aid is designed to ameliorate the more extreme results of such differences. In cases of prolonged illness or death, community members assist the unfortunate family. Mutual aid further emphasizes the *moshav* sense of community: a member ought to consider his fellows and be ready to serve communal as well as personal interests.

Cooperation in the *moshav* is both an ideal and a practical economic system. As an ideal, its aim is "to curb individualism where it tends to become anti-social." [38] While individualism is prized, competition is thought to be wasteful and crass. Cooperation, on the other hand, is considered to be the path to the "good life," since, by cooperating, members reduce friction and also maximize benefits.

In its daily life the *moshav* functions as a typical producers' cooperative. Both purchasing and marketing are cooperatively organized. The *moshav* as a legal entity contracts for capital: for example, long-term loans or equipment are granted to or purchased by the community, which then determines its distribution. Similarly, the community contracts for items such as seeds, water, and fertilizers, usually on short-term credits. Members receive these commodities from a central store, and the amount received is registered in a central bookkeeping system. At harvest time all the families market their goods together. The cash value of the marketed goods is then returned to the community, where it is entered in the bookkeeping ledger. Credits are set against debits—the value of the crops marketed minus the costs of production—and only then are the profits distributed to the producers. Central marketing permits the community loan struc-

[37] *Ibid.*   [38] *Ibid.*, p. 23.

ture to function, since the produce is always under community control.

Dayan calls this arrangement "the mainspring of the economic life of the *moshav*." [39] The system has various practical advantages: for example, cooperative marketing allows for bulk transfer of goods, thereby lowering transportation costs. Similarly, cooperative purchasing eases the loaning of necessary capital. At the same time, these cooperative arrangements have the effect of binding the *moshav* members to one another and thereby heightening their mutual dependence. The *moshav* is, in its daily reality, a highly interdependent social system.

The *moshav* was conceived as a purely democratic community. Indeed, in many respects it well illustrates direct democracy in a small community. Long-range policies are determined at a general meeting where all adult members can voice opinions and cast their votes. Daily management is entrusted to an elected committee. In addition, special committees are charged with various community functions—education, defense, special agricultural problems, and so forth. Since every member has a vote in determining policy, democracy also emphasizes the groups' interdependence.

The first *moshav*, Nahalal, was founded in 1919, eleven years after the establishment of the original *kibbutz*, Dagania. At Nahalal, as in Dagania, the members were both self-selected and screened: that is, the members chose to live together in a *moshav* (many were personal friends), and they also limited membership to persons who shared their values and who seemed socially congenial. Dayan, a member of the Nahalal group, writes that members "were carefully selected, hand-picked, so to speak. Neither pioneer zeal nor agricultural experience alone could win a place in the future *moshav* for a man or woman whom the group did not regard as public spirited and as likely to make a good neigh-

[39] *Ibid.*, p. 28.

bor for a lifetime in a small farming community." [40] The members were also screened for their political outlook: "It was regarded as wise from the first to have the group like-minded on such matters as major Zionist policy or social or economic principles. . . . The group that formed Nahalal . . . were practically all members of Hapoel Hazair, a Socialist-Zionist party not committed to the Marxist theory." [41]

In addition to this tight, original selectivity, the first *moshav* groups often lived together for a training period prior to establishing their own community. During this *garin* (pre-settlement) period, the prospective settlers became intimately acquainted with one another as well as with the rigors of farming. Additional candidates for membership were accepted by group decision: a candidate was required to live in the community for a trial period, and the group later decided whether or not to accept him. In this fashion—by self-selection, ideological and social screening, and pre-settlement training—the first *moshavim* (plural of *moshav*) guaranteed a homogeneous, congenial membership.

Nahalal and the other groups that later based themselves upon the *moshav* pattern were organized as independent communities. The average-sized *moshav* numbered between fifty and a hundred families. Each village maintained its own school, health services, stores, roads, and other services. While their autonomy was prized, various bands of cooperation also developed between the settlements. For example, a national marketing agency (Tnuvah) distributed the settlements' produce, and the villages also organized a purchasing office. In addition, the *moshavim* joined together to form national, political-party affiliated settlement movements.

This analysis has thus far focused upon the establishment of local communities. However, in addition to these settlements, a series of national institutions was then being organized. Political

[40] *Ibid.*, p. 18.   [41] *Ibid.*

direction in the Jewish community was vested in the Jewish Agency, which, during the period of the British mandate, became a virtual "state within a state." [42] The Agency not only carried on a long political struggle but also organized Jewish immigration and directed land settlement. The building of a national worker-led economy was directed by the Histadruth (The General Federation of Labor), which in time included a wide range of institutions that organized and served the new Jewish workers. These two groups possessed broad economic and political powers: they mobilized and controlled large amounts of capital, and they became officially recognized political units.[43]

Direction of the Agency and Histadruth was in the hands of the Jewish elite. Therefore, to a considerable degree, political and economic power was controlled by the pioneer settlers who were actively involved in national affairs. Institutions such as the Histadruth were, at first, informally organized, and their leadership was fluid.[44] In time, however, these groups tended to become increasingly bureaucratized. One of the chief characteristics of the emerging society was the key role of these national institutions and their directing personnel; they quickly assumed a dominant position within the Jewish community.

Although united by common interest and social ties, the national elite was itself often divided.[45] Ideology was paramount and divisions legion. These divisions, highly reminiscent of nineteenth-century Eastern Europe, typically crystallized into rival political parties and into factions within the parties. For example, at various times two, and sometimes three, socialist parties existed; three separate *kibbutz* movements were formed; and the *kibbutz* and *moshav* members within the same party

---

[42] For a description of the organization of the Jewish national institutions, see S. N. Eisenstadt, *The Absorption of Immigrants* (Glencoe: Free Press, 1955), ch. 3.

[43] *Ibid.*, p. 67.   [44] *Ibid.*, p. 80.   [45] *Ibid.*, p. 68.

formed separate interest blocs. The different national institutions
—particularly the Jewish Agency and Histadruth—were themselves based upon party affiliations: their directing personnel was
politically organized and controlled. Thus, not only were national institutions and their personnel powerful, these groups
were themselves directed by political parties.

One of these institutions, the Settlement Department of the
Jewish Agency, is of special importance in this study. First organized in 1920, the Settlement Department was responsible for
directing the development of Jewish agriculture. Its duties
during this era were primarily technical and financial. For
example, the Department's agricultural experts planned each
new agricultural settlement. "Prior to settlement the Planning
Office develops an 'agricultural map' which serves as the basis
for building the village. The soil is tested . . . and a crop program worked out which determines the crops to be grown, the
number of livestock, the number of families that may be settled
in the area, the pace of development, etc." [46]

The Department also developed regional and national farm
plans and provided expert agricultural instruction. In addition,
the Settlement Department was responsible for financing the
new villages. The cost of the farm buildings, irrigation installations, livestock, and so forth, as well as agricultural equipment
and short-term credits, were disbursed by the Department. The
funds distributed were primarily raised by contributions made
by members of overseas Jewish communities. Capital was loaned
to the village at a low rate of interest and was to be paid at some
unstipulated, future date when the community had reached financial solvency. Fairly large sums of money were distributed in
this fashion: for example, between 1920 and 1946 more than
four million pounds had been invested by the Department.[47]

[46] *Report of the 23rd Zionist Congress* (in Hebrew) (Jerusalem:
Jewish Agency, 1950), p. 246.
[47] *Ibid.,* p. 239.

As is apparent from this description, the Settlement Department was an important force in relation to the new *kibbutzim* and *moshavim*. Although each community was autonomous, the villages were dependent upon the Department for loans and expert advice. However, settlement members were typically considered to be of higher status than the Department's workers. As Eisenstadt writes, "those who were most active in realizing the main values and aspirations of Zionist idealism" were granted high status: [48] the settlers were pioneers, while the Department personnel were merely bureaucrats. Moreover, the settlers generally had free access to the key power positions in the Jewish community (many of which they in fact dominated). Thus, while the settlers were dependent upon the Department's funds, they possessed social influence and political power in their relations with the farm planners and experts. These facts are important for understanding later, post-State developments.

Finally, it is important to indicate some of the educational premises that characterized the Jewish community. These are perhaps best illustrated by the *aliyat noar* (youth immigration) program. *Aliyat noar* was a plan in which immigrant youngsters (generally aged 12 to 17) were placed in special training centers where they lived together and received intensive educational training. The children either had no parents (true of many children following the Hitler era), came from broken homes, or were sent by their parents to the children's centers. The children's groups were often located in *kibbutzim* (plural of *kibbutz*), and in some instances special villages were constructed. The educational goals of these centers were those expressed by the national elite: that is, pioneering Socialist-Zionism. What is most striking about *aliyat noar* is its relatively high degree of success in training youngsters in the values implicit in this ideology. In many instances, young people who had no previous attachments to the new value system became re-socialized follow-

[48] Eisenstadt, *op. cit.*, p. 81.

ing intensive training. It will be recalled that the East European
Jews who immigrated to Palestine sought to transform their personalities. *Aliyat noar* may be seen to be an extension of this
reformistic attitude: it is the attempt to change others in the
image of one's own self. This conception of the power of education and reform—and of man's essential plasticity—characterized the elite groups. This ideology was later to have important
consequences for the absorption of new immigrants.[49]

In summary, the foregoing historical analysis has emphasized
selected features of Moroccan Jewish and pre-State Israeli culture. The factors selected became key variables in the immigrants' Israeli experience, and they will, therefore, be more fully
developed in subsequent chapters. Moroccan Jewry was a society in transition, moving quickly from a closed village- and
town-centered tradition to a type of life that was urban, Western, and increasingly differentiated. Traditional patterns of
primary group behavior were being challenged and altered.
Theirs was a mobile society: many of the immigrants had previously migrated to Moroccan towns or cities. Rural or urban social origins and primary group affiliations became especially important in the immigrants' subsequent adjustment to *moshav*
conditions.

The cultural premises and institutional structure of Israeli
society also shaped the immigrants' new life. The ideals of pioneering and cooperation, or the emphasis upon planning and
social reform, were determining factors in their Israeli experience. The Israeli political system, with its stress upon centralized
direction, further conditioned their adjustment.

The cultural context of village development included both
Moroccan and Israeli traditions and the ways in which, over a
period of years, they became adapted to one another.

[49] A description of *aliyat noar* activities is contained in H. Reinhold,
Youth Builds Its House (in Hebrew) (Tel Aviv, 1951).

CHAPTER II

The Immigration Upheaval

IN the previous chapter some general features of Moroccan Jewish and pre-State Israeli culture were sketched out. The historical focus was broad and far-ranging. In the present section, the focus narrows and turns to a consideration of Israeli immigration policies. Moroccan Jewish immigration, as well as the immigrants' subsequent settlement, was planned and directed by Israeli authorities: government policy determined who would immigrate, with whom they settled, and what type of community they lived in initially. The modes of organization discussed in this chapter applied equally to all post-State immigrants— immigrants from, say, Poland, Iraq, or Yemen. However, the distinctive unfolding of Moroccan immigration is closely associated with later events in Israel, and therefore it merits close attention.

Immigration movements may be usefully analyzed in regard to four key questions: what are the principal causes of immigration, who are the immigrants, what information have they regarding their new homes, and what forms of organization does the immigration movement take.[1] Analysis along these lines is

[1] This analysis draws heavily upon several general theories of immigration. See, for example, C. W. Mills, *The Puerto Rican Journey* (New

27

helpful since it focuses upon the characteristics of the immigrant groups, as well as the types of contacts immigrants have with the receiving society. Moreover, the causes of immigration and the composition and communication networks of the immigrant groups are important factors influencing the latter's subsequent absorption.[2]

The causes of Jewish emigration from Morocco are to be found in both "push" and "pull" forces.[3] On the one hand, political and economic crises within Morocco disoriented Jewish life and promoted emigration; on the other hand, many emigrants were attracted to the idea of life in a Jewish State. Immigration movements also generate an internal dynamism: once persons emigrate they draw along their relatives, friends, or acquaintances.[4] Each stage of Moroccan Jewish immigration involved a coupling of these factors: as one observer concluded, immigration was due to "combination of pogroms and messianic fervor." [5]

One principal push toward emigration resulted from violence leveled at the Jewish community. Anti-Jewish terror was first associated with the 1948 Arab-Israeli war. Tension was widespread, and in a series of incidents 43 Jews were killed and 155 injured in two remote Moroccan towns.[6] Although these out-

York: Harpers, 1951); S. N. Eisenstadt, *The Absorption of Immigrants* (Glencoe: Free Press, 1955); S. Lindberg, *The Background to Swedish Migration* (Minneapolis: University of Minnesota Press, 1931); W. Petersen, *Planned Migration* (Berkeley and Los Angeles: University of California Press, 1955).

[2] Eisenstadt stresses particularly the relation between causes of immigration and absorption. His analysis is useful insofar as these factors can be linked. Both Lindberg and Petersen present somewhat more subtle theories of immigration movements.

[3] Mills used these terms in characterizing the Puerto Rican immigration to New York. See Mills, *op. cit.*

[4] See Lindberg, *op. cit.*

[5] *The London Jewish Chronicle*, March 12, 1955, p. 14.

[6] H. Lehrman, "Morocco's Jews Enter the Twentieth Century," *Commentary*, XVIII (1954), 119.

breaks soon abated, they were later replaced by the violence associated with the nationalist movement. Moroccan nationalism was not necessarily anti-Semitic, yet it often led to anti-Jewish outbursts. For example, a correspondent wrote that "an Arab killed a Jewish shopkeeper in Sefrou for selling cigarettes, which, because their distribution is a lucrative French monopoly, the nationalists were boycotting." [7] Terrorism magnified the Jews' anxiety. Each new act of violence encouraged more Jews to choose emigration: "the latest wave of terrorism in Morocco has distinct Jewish—or rather, anti-Jewish—overtones. . . . And significantly, nearly 5,000 Jews registered for immigration to Israel last month." [8] Then too, the Jews' apprehension grew as it became clear that the French would eventually leave Morocco. If Moroccan nationalists permitted anti-Jewish terrorism, how would Jews fare in a future sovereign Morocco? They were "afraid to remain. . . . The fear is endemic, brooding over every *millah* and Jewish home in Morocco." [9]

There were also economic elements in the emigration push. The economic fortunes of Morocco's Jews, never very secure, were further depressed by the dislocations that accompanied the nationalist movement. The *London Jewish Chronicle*'s correspondent in Casablanca wrote that the "poverty-stricken (Jewish) masses have suffered immense hardship from the economic paralysis brought on by the terrorism." [10] Lehrman's comment is even more direct: "The economic character of Moroccan Jewish immigration is clear. . . . They go to Israel to escape poverty, not pogroms." [11]

"Messianic fervor"—a "pull" factor—was another important

[7] H. Lehrman, "Morocco's Jews between Islam and France," *Commentary*, XX (1955), 393.

[8] *The London Jewish Chronicle*, April 6, 1955, p. 1.

[9] Lehrman, "Morocco's Jews between Islam and France," p. 395.

[10] *The London Jewish Chronicle*, March 12, 1955, p. 14.

[11] Lehrman, "Morocco's Jews between Islam and France," p. 395.

element in migration. The creation of Israel touched off a spon-
taneous wave of enthusiasm within each *millah*. Many families
hurried to register for emigration to the "Holy Land," and some
young men enlisted to fight in the Israeli Army.[12] Israeli immigration missions, first established in Morocco in 1948, actively
encouraged this enthusiasm. The Israeli recruiters tended to
paint a glowing image: Israel was described as a land where Jews
lived in freedom and dignity—it was a land of economic growth,
a country that promised happiness and a new life. This image did
not lie, but it was, at best, partial: the hard reality of a poor but
hopeful nation was only rarely expressed.

Once the immigration movement began, it set in motion
forces promoting further immigration. For example, sons who
had left in order to fight in the war encouraged their parents to
immigrate, and the emigration of persons from a city or village
drew others to follow in their path. The emigration stream was
continuous: although there were sudden peaks—usually associated with outbreaks of violence—emigration became a regular
feature of Moroccan Jewish life.

Who were the immigrants? Unfortunately, there are no accurate statistics regarding the immigrant population. It is not possible to reconstruct, for example, the number who were married,
what proportion were city dwellers, or what their occupations
were. In the absence of systematic data one must depend upon
impressionistic analyses. Two general conclusions may be in-
ferred. In the first place, it is probable that approximately
120,000 Moroccan Jews emigrated to Israel between 1948 and

[12] The exact number of Moroccan volunteers is not known, but they
probably numbered between 500 and 1,000. These young people were
the first large Moroccan group to emigrate to Israel. Young, unmarried,
"soldier-types"—and also away from the controls of home and family
—these young men later became something of a problem for the authorities. Indeed, the negative, popular image of "the Moroccan" originates
from this highly selective original group of immigrants.

1956.[13] And second, in contrast with Jewish emigration from Iraq or Yemen, emigration from Morocco was selective: only some Jews chose to emigrate, and of these only certain categories of persons were allowed to embark for Israel.[14]

Observers agree that the emigrants were selected from among the poorer, less acculturated elements of the population.[15] Small shopkeepers, artisans, peddlers, members of the new urban proletariat—the Jews of the traditional *millah* and the small villages—among these masses, emigration held the greatest appeal. Not only had they less to lose, both in economic and cultural terms, they were also closest to traditional Judaism and felt the urge for *aliya* (the Hebrew term for immigration) more strongly.

On the other hand, the wealthy families, as well as those who were more "French," usually decided against emigrating to Israel. For the rich, leaving Morocco meant relinquishing wealth and ease, and many therefore chose to remain. People who were more acculturated saw their future with France or in the new Morocco: as secular persons they did not feel so strongly the magnetism of a Jewish State.[16] Emigration thus brought to a close the process of social division that had begun during the French occupation: the wealthy families remained in the cities while the poor left for Israel.

In addition to self-selection, the Israeli authorities introduced a policy of selective immigrant screening. During the first rush

---

[13] Since the statistical tabulations sometimes refer to "Moroccans" and at other times to "North Africans," it is impossible to give precise figures. This estimate is drawn from tables listed in the publications of the Israeli Central Bureau of Statistics.

[14] On the results of selection in immigration movements see W. Petersen, *op. cit.*, and C. W. Mills, *op. cit.*

[15] Lehrman, "Morocco's Jews between Islam and France," p. 395.

[16] See A. Chouraqui, "North African Jewry Today," *Journal of Jewish Sociology*, I, No. 1.

to emigrate in 1949, nearly all those who registered were accepted. This policy of mass immigration was soon suspended, however, and selective criteria introduced. Selection meant that immigrants had to undergo a general medical examination and that those who were judged physically unfit were not permitted to immigrate. Furthermore, the Jewish Agency officials who directed the program gave preference to younger, physically able persons. Lehrman describes the process as follows:

The rule of thumb seemed to be: for every four or five dependents there had to be one able-bodied wage-earner—usually the father of a family. If the family was larger (North African Jewry is notably prolific), then it might have to find another adult of working age to justify the additional dependents, or prove that an older child was capable of working. In practice, this rule often resulted in the rejection of elderly parents, widows with minor children, and the like.[17]

This accent upon the young may also be seen in the emphasis placed upon youth immigration. In addition to the general emigration program, a special program of youth emigration (*aliyat noar*) was introduced. In most cases, parents registered their children in the program, but in some instances, youngsters seem to have literally run away from home in order to join. Once accepted, the youngsters were organized into special groups and emigrated together, with trained personnel directing them.

Why was selective immigration introduced? Why were some people rejected? The Israeli recruiters were caught between conflicting pressures. On the one hand, they wished to increase the flow of immigrants. As was earlier remarked, the veteran Israeli population believed that they were the vanguard of waves of new immigrants and that once the State was established, Jews would flock to the land. They therefore welcomed potential settlers. There were also more immediate, practical motives: an increased population was needed to bolster the size of Israel's

[17] Lehrman, "Morocco's Jews between Islam and France," p. 397.

army and to settle the barren lands. Moreover, the internal crisis in Morocco appeared to demand immediate emigration: Moroccan Jewry was endangered, and Israel alone was prepared to receive the thousands who wished to leave.

On the other hand, there were powerful pressures for limiting immigration. The Israeli population had increased at an enormous rate between 1948 and 1956: during those years 800,000 immigrants reached Israel, thereby more than doubling the Jewish population.[18] This great influx produced severe social and economic strains: there was an acute shortage of food, homes, and work, and educational and social services were unable to keep pace with the population growth. Nonselective immigration would, it was argued, merely magnify those problems. In addition, since immigration was then taking place from numerous Middle Eastern and European countries, the Israeli authorities gave preference to those countries in which the Jewish communities faced immediate physical danger or where future political conditions were so uncertain that immediate large-scale transfer was necessary. Moroccan Jewry did not always receive top priority: although terrorist outbreaks tended to swell the numbers accepted for immigration, the uncertainty surrounding France's plans to remain in Morocco, and thereby to stabilize the political situation, served to postpone any full-scale population transfer. The Israeli authorities vacillated between alternative policies, but the latter considerations finally led to the adoption of a policy of selective immigration.[19]

[18] See the *Statistical Abstract of Israel*, No. 9, p. 58.

[19] Other factors played a part in the policy of selective immigration. The French officials were interested in keeping the migration flow small. They feared that large-scale Jewish emigration might trigger French emigration in its wake; moreover, they were sensitive to the Arab demands for stopping Jewish immigration. In addition, the Israeli population never seemed reconciled to mass Moroccan immigration. The "Moroccan" stereotype was a negative one, and the public as well as immigration officials were less than enthusiastic regarding the immigration of Moroccan Jewry.

Selective immigration had important consequences for the emigrants. In many cases families were split: since aged parents were often not permitted to emigrate, many families arrived in the new land without an effective head. Younger brothers or sisters emigrated alone, thereby breaking up the circle of family and relatives. These separations often affected the immigrants' subsequent absorption. The screening process itself also had significant results: it represented the immigrants' first contact with Israeli bureaucracy. The emigrants were bewildered by the recruiters' acts—they neither understood the policies, nor were they successfully able to influence them.[20] This situation frequently led to misunderstanding and tension. "The *aliya* registration offices are besieged by pathetically uncomprehending, weeping people who have been rejected as unfit for emigration."[21] These initial bureaucrat-immigrant contacts set a pattern that was later often repeated.

As the immigration movement developed, regular channels of communication were established between prospective immigrants and their informants. The Israeli recruiters were one source of information. For example, letters were sent to local rabbis who, during Sabbath services, read to their congregations glowing accounts of life in Israel. Once immigration began, letters and visits brought increasingly specific information to those who contemplated emigration. Some wealthier families made trial visits to Israel in order to observe conditions at first hand. Moreover, a sizable number of immigrants returned from Israel to Morocco.[22] Many returnees were bitter over their experiences in Israel and spread disquieting stories of their difficulties. A prospective immigrant therefore had various sources of in-

[20] Officials directing the immigration program were normally Jews of European origin who neither spoke nor understood Moroccan Arabic. Local persons filled some of the lower echelon positions.

[21] *The London Jewish Chronicle*, May 8, 1955, p. 1.

[22] Lehrman, "North Africa's Dilemma for American Jewry," *Commentary*, XIX (1955), 227.

formation: the recruiters' descriptions, letters from friends and relatives, or firsthand descriptions from those who had returned. Although these different sources might be expected to produce a realistic image, their major impact seems to have been either confusing or encouraging. Many emigrants selected the more pleasing, optimistic descriptions. Several recalled that they never believed the stories of those who returned: "We thought that they had failed in Israel, and we didn't pay attention to them." It was largely to a "land of myths" that they set out—myths told to them and myths that sprang from their own optimistic imaginations.

The immigration procedure itself involved several stages. A prospective immigrant first registered himself and his family at the Jewish Agency offices.[23] A preliminary medical examination was given, and the candidate was then either accepted or rejected. In most cases no attempt was made to organize the immigrants into large immigrating groups: each individual was registered and processed, and he then proceeded through the various steps without reference to group migration. In some rural areas, however, entire villages were evacuated intact and traveled as a group to Israel, where they were resettled as a unit.[24] But these were special cases and did not apply to most immigrants.

The interval between registration and actual departure varied. The elapsed time depended upon conditions in Israel (the availability of housing, for example) and upon the political climate in Morocco. The waiting period, which often stretched into several months or longer, posed many problems. "A large number of accepted applicants would close their shops or quit their employment, and then have to undergo months of demoralizing idleness while awaiting their turn." [25] Since many sold their

[23] See Lehrman, "Morocco's Jews between Islam and France," *Commentary*, XX (1955), 393.
[24] *Ibid.*, p. 397.   [25] *Ibid.*

goods at reduced prices—the Muslim buyers quickly realized
that the Jews would sell at any price—the lengthy waiting depleted their meager capital. Besides, waiting itself was annoying.
As a result, the registration offices were deluged by impassioned
demonstrations and pleading as the immigrants sought to persuade the officials to hasten their departure.

When a departure date was announced and all the documents
were complete, the immigrant family began its journey. Immigrants were first brought to camps near Casablanca, where they
waited to board ship. Physical conditions in the camps were
simple: each family slept in a single room and ate in a communal
kitchen. Depending upon transportation arrangements, the immigrants either sailed directly from Morocco to Israel or went
first to Marseilles, where they again waited in staging-camps before proceeding to Israel.[26] Although at first each family was
expected to pay something toward expenses, the entire cost was
later normally paid by the Jewish Agency. It was, once again,
the Agency which arranged and controlled the movement of the
many thousands of immigrants.

The brief Mediterranean journey was usually uneventful.
The immigrant ships were crowded, and there was little to do
save to plan, compare notes, and converse. Several aspects of this
portion of the journey are important, however. As was earlier
mentioned, most boatloads were made up of immigrants who
merely chanced to be passengers together. Randomness is significant, since these unrelated people often found themselves later
living together in the new land. Strangers became neighbors,
sometimes under extreme conditions of mutual interdependence.

Furthermore, new types of groups were formed aboard ship.
During the final days of the voyage, Jewish Agency officials cir-
culated among the immigrants in order to register them for settlement. Meetings were arranged, and the Israeli emissaries began
to recruit immigrants. Their task was to encourage as many

[26] See *The London Jewish Chronicle*, November 12, 1954, p. 14.

people as possible to settle in communities allied to their political network. Each shipload included representatives of the different *kibbutz* movements and of the various *moshav* federations.[27] The agents were themselves divided according to a "party key": that is, the proportion of recruiters from a given political party was in accordance with the numerical strength of the party in Israel.[28] The larger the party, the more recruiters and, in theory, the greater the number of adherents it might attract. The competition among recruiters was often fierce, as each sought to enlist larger numbers of immigrants. The recruits—the immigrants—were baffled by this passion: the concept of political party and party ideologies was entirely foreign to them. It was only later that they realized—often with bitterness—that they had become "captives" within a new power system.

Party agents were most successful with those immigrants who had sketchy information and no exact idea of where they wished to settle. With these immigrants it was possible to describe a way of life—the *moshav*, for example—and if convincing enough, register volunteers for settlement. Since competition was extreme, the recruiters tended to paint a glowing image; much was promised, and some immigrants were persuaded. Others, however, resisted the recruiters' pressure. Many requested that they be taken to communities where they had relatives; others asked to be taken to temporary camps, from which they themselves might later arrange their own housing. By the time the boat docked, distribution had already taken place: some immigrants

[27] There are two large *moshav* federations, one associated with the major Labor party, Mapai, and the other with the main religious political party. There are, in addition, four other *moshav* organizations, each associated with smaller political parties. Recruits were enlisted by all six of these groups, but the two large federations organized more than three-quarters of the immigrant villages.

[28] These included only those parties represented in the Zionist Congress, however, and thereby excluded some groups. Moreover, some parties did not establish *moshavim*.

were assigned to new settlements, while others opted to join their families or friends.

Events following the immigrants' landing in Israel may be divided into two periods: the years 1948–1954, during which time most immigrants entered various types of transit camps temporarily; and the post-1954 period, when immigrants were transferred directly from ships to homes in new villages or towns. By 1950 tent camps and *maabarot* (a type of more permanent transit community) were built near the major population and work centers.[29] Living conditions in these communities were extremely primitive. The immigrants' dwellings were temporary buildings made of wood, tin, or asbestos; health, sanitary, and educational facilities were barely adequate. The population of the camps was constantly shifting as newcomers entered and others left. Since the economy could not absorb the sudden influx of new workers, many were jobless, while others found temporary employment in public works projects.[30] Moroccan immigrants who had been artisans or tradesmen discovered that their skills were not needed in the new land, and they were forced to seek employment in unskilled, physical labor. As will later be discussed in greater detail, this shift in role was exceedingly difficult, particularly for the older immigrants. The immigrants were also in a dependent position, dealing continuously with large, bureaucratically organized institutions. "From their first steps in Israel, most of the immigrants were met by various officials . . . whose function it was to deal with them, to direct them to various facilities (housing, furniture, food rations, medical help.)" [31] In short, conditions were chaotic, and it is therefore no wonder that the tent camps and *maabarot* were often places of extreme tension and demoralization.

Immigrant processing after 1954 followed a different pattern. As the pressure of immigration lessened, programs of immediate

[29] See Eisenstadt, *op. cit.*, p. 108.   [30] *Ibid.*, p. 110.
[31] *Ibid.*, p. 135.

settlement were developed. In this "ship to village" program, immigrants were brought directly from a boat to a new village or town. There they found permanent homes prepared for them, and work was guaranteed them for at least several months. Although their immediate housing and work problems were in great measure solved, other problems arose. As had previously been the case, the immigrants were dependent upon the decisions of government groups. Moreover, their range of alternatives was limited: they were brought directly to a small town or farm where their choice of vocation was narrow; their only alternative was to leave, but leaving was normally a lengthy, complex process. They had not chosen these new homes, and thus it was not uncommon for immigrants to refuse to get down off the trucks that brought them to a new, barren countryside.

It is difficult, certainly, to reconstruct an immigrant's first reaction to his adopted land. Yet it is perhaps an understatement to say that many of the Moroccans were shocked by their new life. On the one hand, they felt secure against physical danger, and they sensed a feeling of brotherhood within a total Jewish society. Nevertheless, an immigrant's life was difficult. The land itself seemed bleak and harsh. "I thought it would be like Morocco—but here we found sand and desert, not a rich land," one immigrant later recalled. Their work was often menial, and their physical surroundings meager: it was a poor country, and they entered as members of the lowest social stratum. The immigrants saw too that they lacked power in a social universe dominated by remote government institutions. In all these respects, the situation of Moroccan immigrants was similar to that of immigrants who came from other countries. However, the Moroccans experienced, or thought they experienced, discrimination leveled against them: the fact that they were "Moroccans" did not seem to lend prestige but the very opposite. For example, Shuval has shown that in a mixed housing estate more than 40 per cent of those interviewed listed Moroccans as the

ethnic group "most disliked." [32] The immigrants were bewildered, some were now sorry that they had come, and many
were bitter.

It was not only the immigrants who were shocked, however;
the veteran population was, in turn, disturbed by the new immigrants. The veteran Jewish population, it will be recalled, was
largely composed of European immigrants who tended to share
common symbols. The flood of immigrants pouring into the
country had little in common with their ideology or style of
life: not only were they not inspired by ideals of pioneering,
they were hardly even Western people. Their customs were
very different from those the veteran population had long taken
for granted. Small wonder then that the sense of shock was
deep, and that both the immigrants and the older settlers shared
in it.[33]

The European elite groups reacted to this situation in a characteristic fashion. The idea of reform—the possibility of changing man—was a key aspect of the veteran culture. Thus, European settlers consciously set out to change the immigrants: they
were to be "made" into Israelis and as quickly as possible. The
slogans of the post-State Jewish community were "*klitat aliya*"
and "*mizug ha'galuyot*"—the absorption of immigrants and the
intermixing of ethnic groups. The nature of the crusade for
reform is well illustrated in this statement made by the Israeli
Prime Minister:

We are not just bringing in droves of creatures whom it is enough
to employ, feed and house. These are Jewish men and women, who
will not live by bread alone. This is a people unique of its kind, scattered to all ends of the earth, speaking with many tongues, appren-

---

[32] Judith T. Shuval, "Patterns of Inter-group Tension and Affinity,"
International Social Science Bulletin, VIII, No. 1 (1956), p. 92.

[33] Patai has described certain aspects of this culture shock. See R. Patai,
Israel between East and West (Philadelphia: Jewish Publication Society,
1953).

ticed to alien cultures, splintered into different communities and tribes within the House of Israel. We must again melt down this fantastically diversified community, and cast it afresh in the die of a renewed nationhood. We must break down the barriers of geography and culture, of society and speech, which kept the different sections apart, and endow them with a single language, a single culture, a single citizenship, a single allegiance, with new legislation and new laws. We must give them a new spirit and art, bring them into new social and political orbits and attach them to our past and to our vision of the future.[34]

The main tenets of the culture contact situation are captured in this statement; it indicates some of the expectations the Israeli elite held regarding the immigrants. Expectations were transformed into policies, and the immigrants became the object of concerted programs of sociocultural reform. Throughout the period of heavy immigration, the dominant theory of immigrant absorption was of the "melting pot" variety, as the schools, the army, and other public institutions attempted to re-socialize the immigrants. The immigrants—and this includes, of course, not only Moroccans but the entire post-State immigrant wave—were expected to change, and the pace of change was meant to be rapid. We shall return to this theme again in later chapters.

In reflecting upon this panorama of immigration, it soon becomes apparent that individual desires and national policies often conflicted. For example, immigrants wanted to transfer their entire families—an aged mother or half-blind father, as well as a young son or daughter—whereas the immigration officials often prevented the aged or the ill from leaving. An immigrant from, say, Fez, or from a tiny village near Merrakech planned to join his cousins in Jerusalem or Nathania, but he was dispatched, perforce, to an abandoned Arab village near the border or to a new town in the southern desert. Certainly, much of a material na-

[34] The *Israel Government Yearbook* 5712 (1951/52) (Jerusalem: The Government Printer), p. ix.

ture was provided them—homes, work, schooling for the young, an elaborate system of national insurance, and so forth. Yet, the homes were often in unwanted places, the jobs menial, and insurance meant that monthly deductions were subtracted from meager wages. It is true that they had escaped the indignities and insecurity of Jewish life in Morocco, yet here in the new land they also faced prejudice. Israel did not always appear to be the "Holy Land" of their dreams, at least not at first. The adjustments—to new occupations, different cultural expectations, a new political system—clouded the dream and imposed hardship upon them.

How did the chosen policies effect the immigrants? With the exception of the small number of families who traveled privately, the immigration movement was planned, subsidized, and controlled by Israeli officials. The great mass of immigrants quickly discovered a new world governed by large, bureaucratically organized institutions: they met Jewish Agency emissaries in Casablanca or a small Berber *millah*, met them again aboard ship, and yet again, found administrators dispatching them to new homes and new jobs. An official might be sympathetic, jolly, and efficient, or he might be overwhelmed by work, ill at ease with the hordes of strange-looking, strange-speaking immigrants. In either case, an immigrant needed to learn to cope with Israeli officialdom. The planners and clerks held the key to those things most desired: the scarce, eagerly competed-for resources of housing, jobs, or departure dates. Learning to cope with this new system was a major task; it spawned new attitudes, sometimes leading to extreme forms of behavior.

It was, to be sure, a clumsy system, hastily put together, highly centralized, and often wracked by partisan demands (political party recruiting, for example). Still, the task was enormous, the resources truly scarce, and the results perhaps more than could reasonably be expected. Inevitably, as in all policy matters, the policies chosen often had contradictory results. For example, the selection of young, physically able persons might have been favorable for the immigrants' economic adjustment, but by splitting family groups, this policy often led to the settlers' emotional and social instability. Similarly, the bureaucratic form of absorption procedures developed a sense of paternalism and dependence among the immigrants, while at the same time it offered them economic security in a situation of change. This is not to say that the policies adopted were necessarily in error and that others should have been chosen; every choice leads to new and different dilemmas. It must rather be pointed out that, within this type of system, administrative decisions had a concrete, continuous bearing upon the immigrants' lives.

CHAPTER III

Oren: The First Period

MASS migrations have sometimes been compared to a river current or to an ocean. They are powerful, pulsating movements. Yet upon analysis the floods can be seen to be composed of many tiny streams. The flood divides into smaller units, each of which flows into a different spot, arranging and rearranging itself as it adjusts to a new environment. Thus far we have followed the broad stream, but in this chapter, and henceforth in this study, attention will be mainly focused upon a single, continuous set of events: the development of a Moroccan *moshav.*

Some additional background is, however, still necessary. The settlement program needs to be described first. The process of settlement among Moroccans does not differ significantly from other immigrant groups.[1] As they landed in Israel, the immigrants were channeled into various types of communities. The majority were absorbed within large population centers, cities like Tel Aviv and Haifa, as well as new towns such as Kiryat Shmona and Ofakim. Others were directed to abandoned Arab

[1] In contrast with some other immigrants, however, many Moroccans were directed to the outlying areas. For example, new "development towns" in the north and south have a high proportion of Moroccan immigrants.

villages and towns or to transitional communities such as *maabarot*. Only a minority of immigrants—roughly 17,000, or 14 per cent—were settled in new *moshavim*. It is this minority that concerns us.

In contrast with the pre-State period, the establishment of new villages after 1948 advanced on a mass scale. These communities were seen, in the first place, as a framework for economic absorption: the villages provided a basis for making the immigrants economically productive. Since the majority of Arab peasants had fled during the Israeli-Arab war, large land areas were left untended; new villages established in these regions were an important factor in meeting basic food requirements. Furthermore, creating new villages provided a means for dispersing the population throughout the country, thereby counteracting the tendency to concentrate in a small number of urban centers. The villages also served military functions, particularly in areas such as the Jerusalem corridor, where they were established along the border. Each village was to some degree a military strongpoint. Moreover, as was earlier emphasized, rural life was highly valued by the Israeli elite, and the planning authorities saw the program as having positive social as well as economic results.[2]

The immigrant village program also coincided with the internal "crisis of pioneering" within the veteran elite. The organization of voluntary settlements slackened following the establishment of Israel. Fewer persons from among the veteran population were willing to leave the older cities and towns in order to establish new communities. Eisenstadt explains this change as stemming from "the general weakening of social participation and orientation towards collective values": those who had previously been willing to serve national ideals now wished to satisfy

[2] The settlement process is discussed in greater detail in A. Weingrod, "Administered Communities: Some Characteristics of New Immigrant Villages in Israel," *Economic Development and Cultural Change*, XI, No. 1 (1962), 69–84.

long-deferred personal desires.[3] At the same time, the state
undertook tasks that had formerly been the province of voluntary groups: the post-1948 period saw a growing "formalization,
bureaucratization, and lack of cohesiveness" within Israeli society.[4] The immigrants, directed by the veterans, took up the
"pioneering slack." Paradoxically, it was not the creators of the
ideals but rather the immigrants, untutored and unprepared,
who settled the newer areas.

As in the pre-State period, responsibility for directing colonization fell to the Jewish Agency's Land Settlement Department.
While formerly the Department's role had usually been restricted to technical advice and general capital investment, it
now took almost complete control of the settlement process.
Department planners, in conjunction with various government
ministries and the army, first determined where the new settlements would be situated. Having agreed upon the location, the
Department's staff planned and began to construct the village
itself, and, in conjunction with the various party-affiliated settlement movements, recruited potential settlers. As in all Jewish
settlements, the land itself was leased to the villagers by a national land authority, the Jewish National Fund, and could
thereafter neither be sold nor further divided. Apart from the
land, almost all other items—buildings, farm implements, central
stores, irrigation systems, and so forth—were financed by the
Department. What is more, in addition to investment and technical planning, the Department guided the social development of
each new immigrant community. Instructors were assigned to
each village, and these local officials were, in turn, supervised by
regional and national authorities. In a brief period of years the
Department acquired new personnel—bookkeepers, clerks, driv-
ers, engineers, cattle specialists—as it assumed primary responsibility for the massive colonization project.

[3] S. N. Eisenstadt, *The Absorption of Immigrants* (Glencoe: Free
Press, 1955), p. 132.
[4] *Ibid,* p. 128

The officials directing the settlement project were first faced with the problem of choosing the proper form of settlement. What form of village was most appropriate for the new immigrants? Since the program was to be of a mass, unselected type, the planners agreed that the *moshav,* rather than the *kibbutz,* offered the desirable framework. The *moshav* was considered to demand less intense cooperation and therefore to involve fewer adjustment problems.[5] Following this decision (taken in 1948), recruiters were sent to the immigrant camps.

Our aim then was to settle the abandoned (Arab) villages. Although we knew that these villages were not planned according to our system, there were homes there and we needed to occupy them. The experience would teach us how to proceed in the future. . . . At first we organized mass-meetings in the immigrant camps. . . . Following the meetings we announced that whoever wanted additional information should come to a certain place. How surprised we were—very many were interested! Hundreds gathered around the registration office to receive more detailed information. Settlement groups were quickly organized.[6]

The first immigrant *moshavim* were created in this fashion: immigrants who were enlisted were brought from tent camps to abandoned Arab villages, as well as to new *moshavim* then being built. Later, in the period between 1954 and 1959, settlement groups were formed aboard the immigrant ships, and the prospective settlers were transferred directly to a village. In this way 280 new *moshavim* were founded—more than half the total number of villages formed since the beginning of Jewish colonization.[7]

Organizers of these groups followed several principles of se-

[5] See A. Assaf, *The Moshav Ovdim in Israel* (in Hebrew) (Tel Aviv: Moshav Movement Publications, 1953), especially p. 173.

[6] *Ibid.,* p. 178.

[7] J. Goren, *The Villages of the New Immigrants in Israel, Their Organization and Management* (in Hebrew) (Tel Aviv: Ministry of Agriculture, Agricultural Publications Division, 1960).

lection. First, the potential settlers had to be married. Preference
was given to persons between the ages of twenty and forty
(older men with teen-aged children were also accepted). Prospective settlers were considered to be candidates for membership, and for the first year the settlement movement had the
right to reject them if they proved undesirable. Moreover, the
officials at first consciously strove to form villages composed of
persons from different countries. They theorized that settling
culturally   different   immigrants—Rumanians,   Moroccans,
Yemenites—in the same small community would speed the absorption process. This policy was later changed, however. In
many cases mixed villages were places of extreme tension; the
cultural differences between the settlers magnified their adjustment problems. Since 1952 most villages have been composed of
immigrants from the same country or persons who speak a
common language.

These policies are very different from the pre-State practices
described in Chapter I. Whereas previously *moshavim* were
composed of persons who chose to live with one another and
who underwent intensive preparation before establishing a village, the immigrant *moshavim* were formed administratively,
and the settlers lacked preparation of any kind. In some cases the
villages included traditional social units (such as kinship
groups), but in many instances they were simply composed of
persons who chanced to travel together in the same boat or who
happened to live together in the same tent camp. To put it
differently, group-membership was determined by the planners
rather than the members. Moreover, in almost all cases the settlers had no previous agricultural experience; few had been
farmers in their countries of origin. Generally speaking, they received little training before establishing a village. They were
brought directly from a boat or immigrant camp to a village,
where they immediately began to work.

Immigrant *moshavim* were established throughout the countryside: in the narrow strip facing the Jordan border, the Taanach region near Affula, along the northern coast and interior, and also in the south between Rechovot and Beersheba. The settlement program in the south, the Negev, is especially important and can be usefully examined in detail.

Bordered on the west by the Gaza Strip and Sinai, on the east by the Jordan border, on the north by the settled Israeli agricultural plain, and on the south by the town of Beersheba, the Negev agricultural zone includes an area of roughly 250,000 acres. The dominant natural characteristic is aridness. The Negev is a semidesert with no large underground water supply. Yearly precipitation ranges from nine inches near Beersheba to seventeen inches in the north; and the temperatures range from a mean high of 92° F. to lows of 41° F.[8] The soil composition is principally wind-blown loess. Although potentially fertile, this type of soil needs large amounts of water in order to support intensive cultivation.

Prior to the establishment of Israel much of the Negev was an area of scattered Arab villages and nomadic Bedouin, who, according to Halperin, "extracted a scanty livelihood from their flocks of sheep and cattle and small patches of barley sporadically sown in the desert."[9] The first attempt at Jewish colonization was made in 1946. Inspired largely by political motives, ten *kibbutzim* were established in the region; this quick, overnight settlement was an attempt to claim the region for the Jewish State then forming.[10] These first settlements were experimental: they sought to determine whether colonization was feasible from a defense point of view and whether crops might be successfully grown there.

[8] H. Halperin, *Changing Patterns in Israeli Agriculture* (London: Routledge and Kegan Paul, 1957), p. 3.

[9] *Ibid.*, p. 22.

[10] *Report of the 22nd World Zionist Congress* (in Hebrew) (Jerusalem: Jewish Agency, 1947). Several of these *kibbutzim* were established in the desert zone south of Beersheba.

Once Israel was established, Department and government planners determined to use all efforts to settle the region. Developing the Negev became a major national goal. The experience of the first settlers demonstrated that successful colonization depended upon the availability of a plentiful water supply. A small pipeline bringing water from farther north was laid in 1946; in 1950 and again in 1955 larger pipelines were installed, and comparatively large quantities of water then reached the area. A new Tel Aviv–Beersheba highway was also built, and trunk roads were constructed. Once water and roads were available, community formation proceeded at a rapid pace: electric power lines were connected, farm tracts laid out, and homes constructed. In 1946 there were ten *kibbutzim* in the Negev. Four years later, eight more *kibbutzim* and nine new *moshavim* had been established; the pace of colonization then accelerated so that by 1956 five *kibbutzim* and twenty-five *moshavim* had been added. In a brief span of ten years, fifty-seven new farming communities were built; a new physical framework had been imposed upon the Negev. The cost of the project was very large, amounting to tens of millions of pounds, but the results were certainly impressive. What had been desert was turned into a region potentially capable of growing a variety of crops, attaining high yields, and providing work for thousands of families.

Physical development was, however, only one aspect of the settlement process. The villages had been built, but who would settle in them? The *kibbutzim* in the area were established by voluntary groups drawn from the veteran population. These twenty-three villages were located mainly along the borders, where they formed military as well as socioeconomic outposts. The majority of new communities, however, were immigrant *moshavim:* the settlers were immigrants who had been in camps and *maabarot*, or persons who were brought directly from a ship to a village. More than 80 per cent of these immigrants were Middle Eastern: for the most part, they were Jews from North Africa, Kurdistan, and Yemen (see Table 1).

Oren, the *moshav* described in this study, is situated in the northern Negev, approximately twenty kilometers north of Beersheba. (The name of the village is fictitious, as are the names of villages and persons mentioned subsequently.) The first homes in Oren were built in 1953, and soon thereafter the village was occupied by a group of young Israelis. A year later, however,

Table 1. Negev *moshavim* according to place of origin of settlers (1959) *

Place of origin	No. of villages
Iraq-Iran †	9
Morocco	8
East and Central Europe	5
Tunisia	4
Yemen	3
Egypt	2
Algeria	1
Libya	1
India	1
Total	34

* The information in this table is taken from *A Summary of Settlements Administered by the Settlement Department* (in Hebrew) (Jerusalem: Jewish Agency, Settlement Department, 1959), pp. 1–2.

† Most of the settlers from Iraq and Iran were from Kurdish districts in those countries.

the Israelis left, and in December, 1954, thirty Moroccan families were transferred to the village. This Moroccan group had arrived in Israel several months earlier but had been taken first to a different Negev *moshav*. The reasons for these shifts—the Israeli group's leaving and the Moroccan transfer—reveal important facets of intergroup relations and of the settlement system then evolving.

The Moroccans who settled at Oren arrived in Israel by boat, via Marseilles, in September, 1954. Their landing coincided with the tapering off of immigration from Morocco and the beginning of the ship-to-village program. While aboard ship, the immigrants had registered for settlement in a *moshav*. When they disembarked, they were given a speedy health check and were then dispatched by truck to a Negev *moshav*.

As was often the case, the immigrants were a more or less randomly composed group. With the exception of several pairs of brothers and cousins, none of the immigrants had previously known the others: they were all strangers who met aboard ship. They reached a *moshav* together since they chanced to be traveling on the same boat and because they were selected from among a larger group—several hundred or more—of immigrants aboard ship. The size of the group was determined by the number of vacant homes in the village to which they were sent. In short, the group was formed administratively—by the authorities, rather than by the members themselves.

The immigrants did, however, share certain features. Of the forty families in the original group, only eight had been born or spent most of their lives in major cities; the other thirty-two were from small towns and villages, although some individuals had lived for a time in Casablanca or one of the other cities. None of the immigrants had previously farmed in Morocco; they had all been artisans, peddlers, or merchants. Although several had been comparatively well-off, most arrived with a minimum of clothing and a few household goods: like the majority of immigrants, they were drawn from lower socioeconomic groups. Twenty-nine of the men were between the ages of twenty and thirty-five; eleven were older, and most of these had large families. Two members of the group had formerly been active in Zionist affairs in Morocco. The rest, however, had little information about, or preparation for, the kind of life they were about to begin.

Disembarking from their boat, the forty families climbed into trucks and began the journey from Haifa to the Negev. They traveled at night and therefore saw little of the landscape. The immigrants later recalled the cold of that night on an open truck and what seemed like an unending journey; they were hopeful, but they were also anxious and uncertain of what the future might bring.

The prospective settlers arrived at their destination in the middle of a typically hot, dry morning. The trucks stopped to unload in the central area of a *moshav* called Tzemach. This was to be their home—at least so the settlement officials hoped. Tzemach was one of the first *moshavim* built in the Negev (it was settled in 1950). Situated near an important crossroad, the village was planned to accommodate 100 families. The original settlers were immigrants from Hungary and Rumania. This *moshav* was affiliated with an orthodox religious movement from which it drew its support. In the fall of 1954, however, there were many empty houses in the village: the difficult economic and security situations had depleted the population. The Moroccans who arrived that morning had been sent to replenish the village membership. The fact that Moroccans would live with Europeans was favorably considered by the settlement planners. They theorized that by living together the immigrants would learn from one another, be forced to speak Hebrew, and thereby be absorbed more quickly into the life of the country.

Looking about at the bleak, semidesert landscape, the immigrants at first refused to get down from the trucks. What they saw were several streets of small whitewashed houses, a single store, and irrigation sprinklers spraying water upon rows of crops growing in the distance. Was this the place of their dreams? Eventually they were all coaxed down, and Jewish Agency personnel assigned each family to a house. Every person received a bed, mattress, and blankets, and each family was given food for several days. They had already been promised a parcel of land and agricultural equipment.

What the immigrants did not see, however, were people: where were the other settlers? One of them later recalled that for hours no one else appeared. The veteran settlers, the Hungarians and Rumanians, were apparently cautious regarding their new neighbors. They were not overly enthusiastic about the prospect of living with the newcomers, or so the Moroccans felt. As the veteran community in general, they were committed to the concept of immigrant absorption, but the daily experience of close contact with these seemingly strange Moroccans was disturbing to them. It took hours, therefore, for the Tzemach settlers to come out of their homes and meet their new neighbors.

In the days that followed, the two groups began to make each others' acquaintance. Several of the Moroccans spoke Hebrew and were able to converse with the Europeans. Work had been arranged for them in nearby farms; according to plan, they would at first work as wage laborers and thereby become accustomed to agricultural labor. Several Moroccans were also employed by the European settlers, for whom they picked crops and did various other tasks. Later, in fact, informal agreements were reached whereby several Moroccans transferred their lands to a number of European settlers and in return were permanently employed as wage laborers. This arrangement was advantageous to both parties: the Europeans received additional land and permanent workers, and the Moroccans were freed of responsibility and earned a daily wage. A number of Moroccan women were also employed as domestics in the European households.

For some of the immigrants the situation was satisfactory: they had a home and work. For others within the group, however, the arrangements were far from agreeable. Control of the village was in the hands of the Europeans, who could, it seemed, do as they wished. The Moroccans often felt discriminated against; for example, they were convinced that the store manager was serving the Europeans before them, no matter who stood first in line. Since one often waited in line, this was a continuous source of tension. The religious orthodoxy of the Europeans also disturbed them: the immigrants considered themselves to be religious Jews, but they did not have the European's programmatic zeal. Moreover, the Europeans never really seemed reconciled to the match; they appeared to be waiting for the Moroccans to leave so that a more select group might take their place.

Not more than a few months had passed before most of the Moroccans wished to leave Tzemach. The more influential members of the group were particularly anxious to leave. Although the Moroccans had arrived as strangers, patterns of influence quickly emerged among them. The leaders of the group were several of the older men, particularly those who knew Hebrew. Knowledge of the language was a natural advantage, and soon after landing, these men began to serve as the group's spokesmen. Two brothers named Sephardi were particularly influential spokesmen; not only did they know Hebrew, they had also been active Zionists in Morocco. Much more knowledgeable than the others in regard to Israeli life, they began negotiating with the settlement authorities to transfer the Moroccan group to another village.

The Sephardi brothers met with the Settlement Department officials and, in the name of the Moroccans, asked to be relocated. At one point in their deliberations, they suggested taking some of Tzemach's land, plus land from a neighboring village, in order to create a separate community. This idea was vetoed, however, by the members of the *moshavim* involved. No village would agree to the loss of land. For a time the plans were stalled; no good alternative presented itself, and meanwhile the Moroccans fretted over their lot. They wanted desperately to leave, but who would help them?

Help did come, and their dilemma was resolved, but in an unanticipated (and not well understood) fashion. It was approximately at this point in the group's development that their fortunes became linked with the national Israeli political system. Although small in scale, this incident well illustrates several aspects of the political system the immigrants had entered and how the system influenced them.

Shortly after their arrival at Tzemach, the Moroccans were introduced to a young Israeli who was to be their *madrich,* or instructor. The assignment of instructors to immigrant groups was a standard feature of the settlement program. Enlisted from within the veteran population, a team of instructors was assigned to each village, where they directed economic and administrative affairs and gradually introduced the settlers to farming and co-operative living. Like all instructors, this particular *madrich* had been delegated by a political party, though he received his pay and general direction from the Settlement Department. He visited the Moroccan families regularly and assisted them in meeting the various problems of their new lives—for example, he translated and explained directives, assisted them in their travels to town, and so forth. He was, in addition, responsible for distributing the wages the immigrants earned from their farm work.

What was unusual about this *madrich*'s position was that he was working not only with the Moroccans at Tzemach but also with immigrants in another village. Unlike Tzemach, this other *moshav* and the instructor were both affiliated with a secular socialist party. On most occasions this arrangement would be unacceptable: political parties do not permit rival groups to send delegates into "their" communities, particularly where the disbursement of money is concerned. The fact that the Tzemach settlers did not object indicates that they were not unhappy at the prospect of the Moroccans leaving. For at first subtly, and later more openly, the instructor encouraged the Moroccans to leave for a different *moshav.* He offered to help them in their search. The fact that he distributed money was advantageous. It enhanced his prestige among the immigrants.

One of the Sephardi brothers had brought a truck from Morocco, and he and the instructor traveled in search of a new community. One day they drove to Oren, some five miles away. Here was a *moshav* affiliated with the instructor's party. At that time, Oren was occupied by an Israeli group, but they were about to leave. Sephardi and the instructor inspected the village. The new site appealed to them; here they would be able to build their own separate community. The matter was discussed with the Settlement Department officials, who favored the plan; the Tzemach settlers did not oppose it. Thus, in December, 1954, thirty Moroccan families left Tzemach to take up residence at Oren; ten families decided to remain. This move marked the beginning of Moroccan settlement at Oren.[11]

Before continuing to describe later stages in Oren's formation, it may be useful to reflect upon the events just outlined. How different Oren's formation was from that of the first *moshavim!* Whereas the membership of pre-State *moshavim* was composed of persons who chose to live together and who carefully selected additional candidates, members of the Oren group were strangers banded together by official decision. Moreover, while ideological agreement was a condition for membership in the first *moshavim,* no such criteria of selection entered into Oren's formation, and little attention was given to whether the members shared similar outlooks. The *moshav* format was imposed upon them, and the members were expected to adjust to *moshav* conditions.

Then, too, the brief episode at Tzemach suggests some of the problems of contact between different immigrant groups. Bearers of different traditions, the European settlers and the Moroccan newcomers never established close personal relationships. Even though their contact was brief, it was characterized by friction and misunderstanding rather than by cooperation and

[11] A parallel case which documents ways in which political party recruitment influenced the composition of immigrant villages is contained in D. Willner, "Politics and Change in Israel: The Case of Land Settlement," *Human Organization*, XXIV, No. 1 (1965).

warmth. Notwithstanding the veteran population's stated policy of immigrant absorption, neither group seemed ready to accept or understand the other. Cultural stereotyping and formalized relations, rather than personalized ties, characterized their contacts. (The ten Moroccan families who remained at Tzemach held a peripheral place in that village: they never became active in village affairs, and continued to live there as a separate enclave.)

The immigrants' transfer to Oren points to ways in which newcomers became linked to the Israeli national political system. The group's composition was influenced by the move to Oren —some of the immigrants left Tzemach, but others remained. Moreover, while the immigrants were at first "captives" of the new political system—their transfer to Oren was a coup for the *madrich*'s party—they might be expected to become more adept at understanding and influencing political affairs. They were now associated with the new political system, and as we shall later see, in time some also learned how to manipulate it.

Oren, the immigrants' new home, was built on a natural depression between two small hills; the land itself is flat and gently sloping, and a large wadi runs along the north and western fringes of the village. (The wadi and the area are mentioned in the Bible: "And Abraham . . . sojourned in Gerar." Gen. 20:1.) Two other *moshavim* had previously been built immediately south of the village, less than two hundred yards from Oren. Shikma, the closest village—also settled by immigrants from Morocco—formed the natural center of the three and was the site of a regional school and medical clinic. The third village, Eshed, had a more heterogeneous population: although Moroccans formed the largest group, they were predominantly families who had been in Israel for a longer period of time. All three villages were associated with the same broadly socialist settlement movement.

Oren itself was planned in a general T-shape. A dirt road joined the community to the main asphalt highway. Houses ran along both sides of this road, which then branched out in two directions. At the juncture of the three streets, a series of community buildings had been erected: a general store, produce sheds, a nursery school, a synagogue, and a ritual bath. There were sixty-two houses in the village, and the surrounding fields had been divided into plots of equal size. Eventually, each *moshav* member was to receive twelve *dunams* (approximately three acres) of irrigated land directly behind his house, another ten *dunams* behind these first plots, and a final allocation of ten *dunams*. At the time the Moroccans arrived, the irrigation systems were being installed in the plots behind the settlers' homes.

The settlers' first problem concerned their work: how would they learn to farm? In order to ease the transition to independent farming, the Department officials proposed instituting a plantation-type system. According to this plan, the village lands would not be divided immediately among the families, but instead the crops would be grown in a single large area and the settlers employed as wage laborers. It was argued that in this way the new farmers would not bear immediate responsibility for profit and loss yet would gradually learn agricultural skills. The settlers agreed to the suggestion; in fact, most of them desired it. The settlement movement with which Oren was associated also agreed. According to the arrangement, the Department was to lend equipment and credit, the settlement movement was to provide the instructors, and the immigrants were to supply the manpower.

From their first day at Oren, the settlers were thus guaranteed an income. Under the direction of the instructors they went out to work in the fields. The work system was relatively simple. There were three instructors in the village; two were responsible for the farm work, while the third managed the village's economic affairs. After consultations with Department experts, the instructors decided upon a crop rotation. Next, they ordered tractors which prepared the land and spread seed and fertilizers.

Cultivation, irrigating, and harvesting were then done by the settlers, working under the direction of the instructors. Each morning an instructor met his workers, explained the work to them, and then supervised their labor.

This system, while theoretically efficient, posed many difficulties. For one thing it placed great power in the hands of the instructors. They could, for example, reward certain settlers by assigning better work to them, leaving the dull or difficult tasks to others. The labor assignment soon became a main source of tension; some workers complained bitterly of favoritism. Similarly, while it was desirable to rotate persons in each of the jobs so that everyone would have a chance to learn the various skills, it became apparent that some men were more adept than others; soon these men were assigned permanent jobs (for example, arranging the irrigation system). Permanent jobs were considered an advantage and, when awarded, provoked quarrels. In addition, there was the problem of determining work norms. What constituted a "day's work"? First the instructors asked the most adept worker to run through a "trial day." Having thereby established an extreme, they lowered it to get an average. This system was also a source of complaint; the workers always sought to lower the norms.

The instructors thus found themselves in an uncomfortable position: while ostensibly teachers, they increasingly became overseers. They were torn between their own ideals of democracy and equality, and the demands for rational, cheap production. This situation, in which those in control were seemingly forced to adopt techniques and attitudes at odds with their own ideals, never ceased to trouble the settlement authorities. Relations between instructors and settlers became strained, although some of the Moroccans—the better physical workers and those who more quickly adapted to the system—enjoyed warm ties with the Israelis.

Despite these tensions, many immigrants profited from their

work. The larger families in particular thrived; at harvest time they would send six or seven family members to work. It was, in a way, a "golden period": the settlers had no financial responsibility, and they were guaranteed work. While the plantation itself (that is, the Settlement Department) probably lost money, most of the settlers profited. This situation had important consequences. The settlers were not involved in the community's financial or technical planning: that was the instructors' task. They had no accurate information regarding the village's finances. They perceived a large capital-dispensing institution— the Settlement Department—which seemed to have limitless funds and great influence. Paternalism and dependence were thus implied features of their new social situation, and the immigrants' perceptions and actions responded accordingly.

During this early stage in Oren's development, only half the houses were occupied by new immigrants; three houses were occupied by the instructors, while about twenty of the original Israeli group still remained in the village. By the summer of 1955, however, all the Israelis had left Oren for a border settlement farther north. The reasons for this move are complex. The main motivation seems to have been that while Oren was in a comparatively safe area and therefore could be occupied by new immigrants, the more dangerous border villages could be settled only by persons with military experience. Although pressure was put on the Israelis to remain at Oren—for example, influential party members met with the Israeli group and argued that they should remain with the newcomers—in the end, the argument of "immigrant absorption" was overruled by other considerations.

The houses left vacant by the Israelis were soon occupied. New settlers arrived, asked permission to join the community, and were accepted. With the exception of two Tunisian families, they were all recent immigrants from Morocco. Moreover, unlike the original group, the newcomers were all persons who had relatives in Oren or in the neighboring Moroccan *moshav*. These kinsmen, who came singly or in small groups, were encouraged by their relatives to join the village: they were attracted by the steady work on the plantation, the freedom from responsibility, and the available homes. Then, too, they wished to live together with their relatives. At the same time, two larger groups of kin asked permission to join the village and were accepted. One of these groups numbered ten families and the other fourteen. In a brief time most of the sixty-two homes were filled.

This "chain migration" had significance far beyond the growth in village population: in effect, it changed the village's social structure. Whereas the original group had been composed of strangers, within a year after settling at Oren nearly every settler had relatives in the village (see Table 2). This shift gave some individuals powerful social support while isolating others. Unplanned and almost unnoticed, this change soon had far-reaching consequences.

Table 2. Composition of Oren by family membership (1957)

Type of group	No. of families
Small kin units	
(one to four kinsmen)	21
Dehan families	14
Levi families	10
Extended family	4
No kinsmen	8
Empty homes	5
Total	62

The plantation had been the settlers' introduction to agriculture. Soon, they were also introduced to the *moshav* political system. According to *moshav* theory, a village is governed by an elected committee, chosen at a general meeting. Several months after the Moroccans reached Oren, the instructor organized a community meeting, and a committee was elected. This first committee was composed of older men, most of whom had held minor positions of prestige in Morocco. Membership on the committee changed frequently, however, since recurring village tensions brought opposing groups into conflict. The moving spirit in the village was still, however, Chaim Sephardi. His knowledge of Hebrew and flair for leadership made him the most influential person among the immigrants. Unlike the others, however, he did not work on the farm. At first he sought work with his truck, but later he aspired to become the village's paid secretary.

The idea of the committee had been to introduce the Moroccans to self-government and to consult with them regarding the village's recurring problems. In the future, the instructors said, the settlers would be independent, and they had to learn to manage their own affairs. In actuality, however, all important decisions were taken by the instructors. Sephardi was dissatisfied with this relationship: he wanted equality with them and wished to participate in framing policies. Persistent quarrels broke out between Sephardi and the instructors. Sephardi desired to lead; he had his own ideas, and they were not always compatible with the instructors' plans. To the *madrichim* (plural of *madrich*), he was a nuisance and troublemaker. The instructors thought they had come to Oren to teach a new way of life; they were not content to be dependent upon older leaders, particularly upon those who did not themselves work. (The nature of this conflict may be better appreciated if the ages of the "contestants" are indicated: the instructors were in their middle twenties, while Sephardi was forty-six, the father of eight children.)

This frequently bitter struggle soon ended. Sephardi's leadership was not always recognized by the settlers themselves: there were daily tensions, and he was often blamed. Soon several newcomers, younger men, challenged his leadership. The instructors immediately supported these men. This support was decisive, since the instructors' attitude bore considerable weight. Finally,

Sephardi announced at a general meeting that he would no longer take part in community affairs: he could no longer challenge the instructors. He found work outside the village, and leadership passed on to others.

The dilemmas of direction are, once again, well illustrated by these incidents. The instructors had desired indigenous community leadership. Yet for them, Sephardi, who showed no intention of becoming a farmer, represented the "old ways." By supporting the younger settlers, they sought to transfer authority to those who were presumably more "progressive"— immigrants who had begun to adjust to the new life of work.

Leadership was then taken over by one of the kinship groups: the Levi families. Young, ambitious, and excellent workers, the Levis captured all of the key village positions: the elder uncle became the village rabbi, an older brother, the village secretary, and another brother, the produce manager. These were all permanent jobs, and each included a monthly salary. By dominating the committee, they were able to influence important decisions: for example, all equipment and funds allotted to the village were funneled through the committee, and the Levis were able to influence the distribution of capital. This was an obvious advantage, and the Levis maintained their control through shrewd alliances and a system of "patronage." The Dehan families, the largest kinship group, became their chief opposition. Pitted against one another, these two kinship groups waged a long struggle for political control. During the next five years, there were innumerable squabbles, threats, mediations, and a final wild melee. The community was split into two factions, a condition that daily influenced the course of events.

The plantation arrangement continued through the summer and fall of 1955. Increasingly, however, some settlers grew dissatisfied with this system; many requested that the plantation be dissolved and the land divided among them. Those who demanded parcelization reasoned that if they were able to profit from a plantation arrangement, they would reap even greater rewards if they themselves received the profits they imagined the farm managers and Settlement Department were realizing. Rather reluctantly, the Department agreed to divide the land. While skeptical of the settlers' ability to achieve economic independence, their losses on the farm were so heavy that the authorities were willing to turn the land over to the settlers. Besides, village independence was the goal of the entire enterprise. Thus, in December, 1955, the lands were parceled out. A few settlers —those who had opposed parcelization—left the village. The village population then numbered 328 persons, of whom 175 were below the age of seventeen. Table 8 on page 186 lists the age distribution in 1956.

During this first year the settlers received their induction into their adopted society: they began to farm, met other Israelis, reestablished relationships with old Moroccan friends, and slowly began to understand the cultural idiom of the new land. It was, in retrospect, a useful period: the settlers were more or less guaranteed an income, and some did begin to master the farming techniques. To be sure, there were crises, but there was also economic security of a kind. The village's population grew and changed in character—nearly all of the sixty-two homes were occupied, and the new members were mainly kinsmen who had rejoined their relatives. A different type of social system was thereby formed. New patterns of influence and leadership emerged, both as a response to new physical conditions and as a result of interaction between the settlers and the Department officials. At the end of the first year, the introductory plantation phase was replaced by family-based farming and community-wide cooperation.

Before going on to consider the next phase, it may be well to take a wider perspective of the events described above. How does Oren's formation and initial development compare with other immigrant villages? It is surely difficult to generalize re-

garding these matters: each village was unique, and the course of
development in each community had many special aspects. Nevertheless, it will be useful to compare briefly Oren's formation
with that of the neighboring Moroccan village, Shikma.

Shikma's history dates back to 1953 when twenty-six Moroccan families were sent to a transit center in the south of Israel.[12]
These families had traveled together on the same boat and were
selected from among an entire shipload to be sent to a transit
camp. Most of the family members shared an urban background: twenty-three were from Fez, Merrakech, Casablanca,
and Safé, and only three were from rural areas. In Israel the
immigrants were contacted by a young Moroccan who had been
active in Zionist affairs in Casablanca and who had emigrated to
Israel in 1949. This young man, named Machlouf, was at that
time seeking to organize a Moroccan group for settlement in a
moshav. He explained his plans to the families in the transit
camp. After many discussions with the immigrants and the settlement officials, it was finally decided to transfer the immigrants
to Shikma. In the summer of 1953, the twenty-six families
moved into newly constructed homes in Shikma. After their arrival, another family joined the village. The head of this new
family, Daniel, had arrived in Israel in 1948, as part of the first
wave of Moroccan immigrants. Daniel was well versed in the
new Israeli situation and soon commanded authority among the
immigrants. He and Machlouf subsequently became dominant
personalities in the emerging community. Indeed, Nomi Navo,
who studied this village, writes that these "two personalities
. . . are of immense importance to the social history and to the
present social and political picture of Shikma." [13]

The social composition of Shikma later changed drastically.

[12] N. Navo, *Shikma: A Village in the Western Negev* (Jewish Agency,
Settlement Department, mimeo, 1961). My understanding of this village
is mainly based upon Navo's study, and I would like to express my
thanks to her for the use of the data and its interpretation.
[13] *Ibid.,* p. 6.

While the original settlement group was composed of immigrants from urban Moroccan areas, the population later came to include large numbers of persons from rural regions. For example, of the forty-four settlers who joined the village between 1954 and 1961, twenty-four came from rural areas and twenty from towns. Moreover, during this same period there was a general exodus of urban settlers: Navo notes that of the twenty-eight villagers who left Shikma between 1953 and 1961, twenty-six were families with urban backgrounds.[14] Selective internal migration—both to Shikma and from the village to other communities—resulted in a community equally divided between persons with rural and urban backgrounds: of the forty-eight families living there in 1961, twenty-four came from rural regions and another twenty-four from towns.

These changes in personnel also involved changes in village social structure. What distinguished the rural settlers was their organization into kinship units: all but three of the rural families were joined into such groups. Ten of the rural settlers belonged to a single unit, while another eleven families were organized into either extended families or smaller kinship clusters (several cousins or brothers-in-law, for example). For the most part, the urban settlers lacked such ties: nineteen of the twenty-four had no family or kinship ties in the village. It is particularly important to note the large number of persons lacking close ties of any kind: these included twenty-four of the total of forty-eight families.

After this brief survey of information regarding Shikma's formation and the composition of its population, a comparison with Oren leads to several important conclusions.

The settlement process in the two villages was roughly similar: both were composed of unselected Moroccan immigrants, and, in both, the settlers arrived in their village without previous preparation. The population of the two communities changed

[14] Ibid, p. 8.

rapidly during the first year. Parallel activities of the Settlement Department—the assignment of instructors, capital investments, loans, and so forth—were initiated in the two communities. On the other hand, the social composition of the villages and their distribution of authority, differed significantly. Unlike Oren, where nearly all of the settlers were from rural Moroccan areas and almost all had kinsmen living in the village, the Shikma settlers included immigrants from both rural and urban areas, and 50 per cent of the settlers had no kinsmen in the village. Moreover, the two leaders of the Shikma community, Machlouf and Daniel, polarized that community in a manner much different from the allocation of authority at Oren. These variables— urban or rural origins, the presence of kinship units, and the distribution of authority—had a significant impact upon the villages' subsequent development, as we shall see later.

CHAPTER IV

Contexts of Village Life

THE period of the plantation was brief, lasting only a year. The second phase of Oren's development—the years between 1955 and 1960—was marked by the settlers' entrance into family-based farming and community-wide cooperation. The following three chapters consider events during this "middle phase," the period when the immigrants, often painfully and rarely cheerfully, sought to adjust to their new conditions.

Becoming a Farmer

None of the settlers at Oren had formerly been farmers; farming in Morocco, like physical labor in general, was a Muslim monopoly. Those who had grown up in rural areas were, to some extent at least, familiar with animals and crops. Two of the younger men had also been members of *aliyat noar* groups and received some agricultural training. For the other settlers, however, everything about their lives as farmers was new and different.

The transition from a shopkeeper's or artisan's routine to a life of physical labor involved a series of crises. The settlers were not accustomed to physical exertion. Their bodies were not prepared for the strain and much more important, neither were their attitudes or feelings. In time, muscles hardened and sinews became powerful; after months of farm work, most settlers were physically able to work long hours in difficult tasks. Nevertheless, the shift to farming implied a more difficult adjustment—an almost total reorientation of the settler's status image.

"Look at me now," a settler remarked one day as he returned from his fields. "What do you see? Not a Jew! A Jew isn't covered with dirt, a Jew doesn't wear a torn shirt and have shoes caked with mud. I'm an Arab now, not a Jew!" Comments such as this were voiced frequently. They were cries of despair. The settlers associated farming with Muslims; physical labor was for them synonymous with low status. Their new role as a farmer did not bestow honor, but rather degraded what was held to be a man's proper status. The settlers had no ideology of labor, no natural ties to soil and work. Quite the opposite was in fact true: physical labor was thought to be damaging, work in the hot sun, harmful. In becoming a farmer a man struggled with some of his most cherished notions and cultural ideals. Even those who became successful found their lot somehow humiliating; they often wished to pursue a more familiar, honored occupation.

There are other facets to this crisis. The men were accustomed to working with or near others, but much of the work in the fields was done independently. For some of the settlers this was a difficult adjustment. "I thought I would go crazy out there," one settler explained. "I was in the fields hoeing for hour after hour. There was no one to talk to, and so finally I just threw down my hoe and left. How can you work by yourself all the time?"

The farming schedule itself imposed tensions. The pace was difficult. "In Morocco I would close my shop in the afternoon. If there were no customers I would sit or visit with my friends. We would often go to visit relatives, sometimes for days and even weeks. But how can I leave here? If I go away, who will care for my fields? Here I get up in the morning when it is still dark outside, and in the middle of the night I have to get out of bed to turn off the sprinklers. There is never any break." Life in Morocco may not have been so idyllic, and not all the settlers worked so consistently. Yet the unrelenting rhythm of farm work was one of the most difficult aspects of the new life.

To grow crops requires many different acts. Planting seeds, spreading fertilizers, hoeing, and irrigating are part of a pattern in which men invest their labor and skill in the hope of plentiful harvests. Not all of the new settlers successfully mastered the skills, and not all understood the farming process. Many did not learn how to organize their work efficiently; they performed their chores in a clumsy fashion. Moreover, not everyone understood that good yields depended upon adequate and proper investment of time and materials. For example, some settlers would irrigate for two hours instead of the required four or spread less than the required amounts of fertilizer; ostensibly, one saved money by spreading less fertilizer or by irrigating for shorter periods of time. That improper farming practices resulted in low yields was not yet fully appreciated.

The settlers had had their first farming experience while working as wage earners on the plantation. While it is difficult to know, particularly in retrospect, how they learned new attitudes and skills, the plantation experience was for many a useful introduction to physical labor and the intricacies of farming. Some settlers learned to rise early in the morning and to work conscientiously; they learned the "tricks" of hoeing and cultivating, and the proper times and ways to irrigate. Many others, however, learned very little; they disliked work in the hot sun and were confused by the new techniques.

Working one's own land was in any event quite different. On the plantation each settler had worked under continual direction, following the instructor's orders; although they later continued to receive advice, a settler working his own land was free to accept or reject the instructor's suggestions. While many aspects of the farming system were controlled by the *madrich*, each settler set his own pace. All the nonmechanized farming tasks were the settler's responsibility. Profit and loss were, in theory, the fruits of his own labor.

If one did learn the new skills, one learned by experience. A settler learned to grow tomatoes, if at all, after four or five seasons. In time and with experience, he learned when to plant seeds, when and how to spread fertilizer, the proper times to irrigate, when to hoe, how to set up the poles and lines, how to recognize the signs of disease, and when to begin the harvest. Able instructors offered useful hints and directions, but the real learning, if it occurred at all, was in the fields.

The degree of success in farming varied greatly: some settlers achieved handsome yields while others failed completely. Several factors are associated with success in farming. Youth is an advantage, and the younger people at Oren were among the better farmers. The young, who tended to be agile and strong, had an edge over those who were older and tired easily. They also had closer ties with the instructors; more "progressive" than their elders, they were responsive to suggestion and advice. Moreover, for them the adjustment to physical labor was less of a crisis: they had fewer ties with the older tradition.

A second factor associated with successful farming was membership in a large family or kinship group. A man with a large family was potentially able to mobilize many hands for farm work; a settler with five or six teen-age or even younger children could weed his crops more quickly and efficiently than the settler who had no claim upon the labor of others. Membership in a kinship group had similar advantages, since kinsmen often cooperated in performing the farm chores.

There were, however, striking differences between persons falling into these broad categories: not all of the younger men became successful farmers, and not all of the large family or kin groups were able to maintain inner discipline and cooperation. Within a single family one brother perhaps made a better adjustment than the others; some of the young were stronger or more intelligent than the others, and some were more willing to accept a farmer's role. Those who had received agricultural or army training tended to make the most successful adjustment. Similarly, some fathers were able to control their sons and daughters within the work system, while in other cases the children rebelled. In order to maintain cooperation, parents had to establish a delicate balance between their authority and direction, on the one hand, and the delegation of responsibility and reward on the other. Not all parents were able to find this "golden mean." In general, however, youth and family size were associated with success in farming; the younger men and those who could mobilize assistance made better adjustments. These men then became models for the rest of the village: their agricultural practices were often watched and copied.

Farming was one of the most difficult aspects of the settlers' lives. They had no traditions of land and work. If they had sentiments regarding the soil, they were damning rather than ennobling. Most found their lot hard and lacking in reward; there was no inspiration or accepted ideology that glamorized a farmer's life. The majority would have left farming if they could have. They farmed since they had no real alternative, and many hoped that if they were successful, they would have sufficient funds to leave for the city. Although these attitudes later changed—as will be shown in the final chapter—during this phase farming as a way of life had yet to take firm root.

Village Life

All the homes built at Oren were originally of equal size; each included two rooms, one of which was a kitchen, the other a sitting-sleeping room. (The enclosed area totaled 35 square meters.) For most families this meant cramped conditions: the rooms were small, most families had several children, and some had older parents living with them. Additional rooms were later built for those who had more than five children; in most cases a bedroom and small shower room were added on, and in some instances a third room was built. Building these additions was usually a lengthy process, and often, large families were forced to crowd together for months and sometimes years.

Many homes were furnished in almost identical fashion. The cement walls were whitewashed and then finished with colored designs. The kitchen was planned with the sink facing one end and a shower the other. The women cooked on kerosene burners and usually served in the kitchen. Many families put a simple wooden table and several chairs in the kitchen area, but the family usually ate sitting on the floor, alongside the table and chairs. It seemed more convenient to eat while sitting near the burner.

One of the rooms was typically arranged as a sitting-sleeping room. Many acquired a dining table and several chairs. The table was invariably covered by a glass, beneath which wedding pictures and family photos were displayed. The family ate there only on special occasions. Along the wall a radio was usually to be seen on a small table. Every family purchased a radio; as long as it was in working order, the settlers listened to the news in Hebrew, or more commonly, to Arabic music. (The radios were elaborate, and once broken, bringing them to the city for repair was a complicated chore; thus a sizable proportion were always out of order.) A third fixture of most sitting rooms was an ice box; during the summer ice was delivered several times a week and was the only way to preserve food. Several metal beds were also arranged along the walls, and here the children slept.

The second room was normally the parents' bedroom. It contained a large storage cabinet for clothing, a double bed, and a crib. There were no doors between rooms, and the doorways were covered by patterned curtains.

Turning next to the farm area, each settler's farm plot was standardized and similar to his neighbor's. Several small buildings were located behind each home: the privy, a barn for cattle, and a small granary. The main twelve-*dunam* farm plot was laid out behind these outbuildings. A central water pipe ran the length of the field, and served two neighbors. At intervals along this pipe protruded nozzles to which aluminum irrigation pipes were attached. Rows of vegetables and industrial crops extended across each plot; these included cotton, sugar beets, peanuts, potatoes, and tomatoes. In most cases, these crops were planted some distance behind the settler's house. A family garden area was generally located between the farm buildings and the main fields. It was meant to supply home needs. Some settlers even obtained seeds from Morocco and planted small quantities of vegetables that were not readily available in Israel (broccoli and red peppers, for example). These family gardens often became quite sizeable, since many settlers planted large areas of crops which they marketed privately.

The work day normally began at 6 or 7 A.M. During the spring and summer months (from March to October) men rose earlier in order to work in the cool of the morning. Returning from the fields at 9 or 10 A.M., they ate a large breakfast and then went back to work. The main meal was usually taken in the middle of the day and was followed by a long siesta. The men returned to work at 3 or 4 in the afternoon and remained in the fields until sunset. Although most families worked their plots independently and without interruption, neighbors working in adjoining fields sometimes paused to visit. The general store and packing shed were the usual places of informal gathering, however. Whenever a number of men gathered together, there was the likelihood of gossip and an exchange of grievances. Kinsmen and neighbors often visited in the evenings, although most settlers retired early in order to be prepared for the following day's work.

The demands of tending crops kept most men tightly bound to their farm plots; tending the crops was their primary responsibility. Women had a number of different tasks. In the first place, a woman cared for her home and children. She washed the floors, prepared the meals, shopped at the general store, mended the clothes, and looked after the few chickens or sheep that circled about most homes. She nursed and cared for the infants and young children. In addition to these household chores, many women worked in the fields. Hoeing was typically done by women. In most families, the family garden plot was also the woman's responsibility.

Children began to assume responsibilities at an early age. Children over the age of three were in school for part of the day. Those from three to six went to the local nursery school each morning; younger children were sometimes sent along, so that the mothers were free to attend to their chores. Children between the ages of six and fourteen attended classes in the local regional school. After school they had various tasks. For example, young girls helped their mother to care for the infants; youngsters of seven or eight were often seen looking after two or three younger sisters or brothers while their mother was away in the fields. The boys worked with their fathers—hoeing, picking, moving the irrigation pipe, or driving the horse and wagon. As they grew older, they began to take greater responsibility. The older boys—those who had finished school and were not yet drafted into the army—often carried a major burden of farm work.

There are two main crop seasons in the Negev: one begins after the winter rains (in late February or March) and the other in September-October. Before preparing the ground, the settlers were notified of the crops to be planted. "Notification" might mean simply a sign posted in the general store, or there might be a planning meeting with some of the Settlement Department experts. A spring crop program at that time typically included a *dunam*-and-a-half each of potatoes and onions, a *dunam* of tomatoes, four *dunam* of cotton, three *dunam* of maize, and a *dunam* of peanuts. When the crop program was announced, the minimum price the settlers might expect to receive was also posted. Both the allotment and the prices were fixed by a national, quasi-governmental marketing board.

Following the announcement of the crop program, the village instructor ordered tractors from the regional tractor centers; the machines plowed each individual plot, preparing it for planting. For some crops, the settler had to go over the soil again with a horse and clodbreaker, in order to pulverize the large chunks of earth. Once the soil was prepared, seed and fertilizer were spread; this was usually done by hand, since the plots were too small for mechanized seeding. Cultivation and irrigation then began. Irrigation was often done at night, after the winds had died down. It was a lonely task, and the village watchmen joined the settler who arose to move his pipe, in order to protect him from marauders. (This was particularly true in the "pre-Sinai campaign" period when Arab terrorists from Jordan or the Gaza Strip were frequently in the area. Following 1957 this danger largely subsided.)

Sowing, cultivating, and harvesting were usually done by an entire family. Although some wives resented it, most submitted to it. If there were aged parents or relatives in the household—a grandfather or older aunt—they too were recruited to help. At harvest time, the entire family went out to the fields to pick the tomatoes or cotton. The crops were then brought to a central shed, where they were weighed and later shipped to market.

Families had several other legitimate sources of income in addition to farming. During the winter rains, when there was little farm work, the Settlement Department provided funds for village public works (planting trees, digging drainage lines, spraying against insects and pests, and so forth). Nightly guard duty, organized by the army, was also remunerated. Cattle rais-

ing was introduced in the village in 1958. The settlement movement with which Oren was affiliated provided loans enabling
the settlers to purchase beef cattle. Several shepherds were hired
to care for the village herd, which went out to pasture each
morning and returned to the individual sheds at night.

One routine of village life revolved about this agricultural
cycle—the rhythm of seasons, planting and harvesting. Another
routine followed the religious-ceremonial cycle. Every Sabbath
the men gathered together to pray in the village synagogue; this
regular gathering played an important role in the political as
well as social life of the community. With the exception of several younger boys, nearly all of the men regularly attended the
Sabbath prayers. Some of the older men prayed each evening,
but most came to the synagogue only on the Sabbath. Religious
festivals were celebrated by each family; the observance was
traditional, although the regional school sometimes organized
"modern" celebrations. For example, *Rosh Ha'Shana,* the observance of the New Year, was celebrated in traditional fashion.
Chanuka, the Feast of Lights, was also celebrated traditionally;
but, in addition, during *Chanuka* the school children, directed
by their teachers, recited poems and sang and danced modern Israeli dances before an audience of their parents and older siblings.

A marriage or birth in the village was an event of general interest. These occasions were looked forward to with keen antici-
pation; kinsmen and friends traveled from other communities to
join in the celebrations. Weddings were especially happy events:
the entire village was usually invited and a sense of well-being
prevailed.

Each Saturday night, a local entrepreneur brought a film to
Oren, and the whole village usually attended the showing. Although most people did not understand the language of the film
(occasionally there was a French film which a few settlers understood) everyone looked forward to this weekly treat. Unless

one went to Beersheba for an evening—a journey rarely made, and then only by the younger settlers—the movie was the only form of regular entertainment. Secular national holidays, such as Israel's Independence Day, were only partially celebrated; these holiday events were poorly organized, and the settlers themselves had no informal means of celebration. National events were sometimes followed on the radio, but the settlers rarely understood the broadcasts, and their participation was limited.

The immigrants responded variously to village life. Ameliah, who had been a storekeeper in Casablanca, found the change to be a refreshing experience; he was the "village philosopher," and he worried over Man and his condition. However, Ameliah was in the minority. Like most "village philosophers," he was not appreciated by his neighbors, and his ideas were not taken seriously. Most of the settlers found their new life dull and confining: apart from the Saturday night movie and an occasional wedding, there was little for them to do except work, visit with friends, and participate in the often frenzied village politics. Oren was a small community numbering less then sixty families, distant from towns and the life of the city. There was only one store in the village, and its stock was meager. A man or woman who wished to dress up discovered that he or she had no place to go; recreational activities such as social dancing or soccer were sporadically attempted but never sustained. The younger people felt especially limited. "There is nothing to do here, only work and sleep. I'm tired of seeing the same faces," they complained. The settlers thus struggled to adjust to the narrow social limits of a small farming community.

Oren as a Moshav: *Cooperative Farming*

Oren was organized according to the model of the classic *moshav*. As in the first cooperative villages, each farmer was an independent producer, decisions were made democratically, and purchasing and marketing were organized cooperatively.

Cooperative farming, insofar as it was practiced, meant that the settlers were joined together within a system of centralized loans and payments. The system was, in outline, relatively simple. Since the settlers had no capital of their own, the Settlement Department and other allied national institutions (notably Mekorot, the national water company, and Ha'Mashbir Ha'Merkazi, agricultural supply agency of the Histadruth) extended credits to the village. These credits, in the form of seed, water, fertilizer and monthly cash loans, were granted against the crops the settlers grew: the settlers were obliged to repay the loans following the harvest. Every settler was eligible to receive loans; the sole requirement was that he show good faith in making repayment and that the Department's crop schedule be followed. Unless a settler had independent financial resources —no one at Oren had cash reserves—he could not grow crops of his own choice; credit was extended only to those who agreed to follow the Department's crop program.

There are several reasons for this procedure. Crop controls were an attempt to check agricultural surplus; overproduction, with the attendant depressed prices and crop dumping, was a constant threat. Moreover, an imposed rotation meant that the soil's richness would not become depleted by replanting the same crop each year. A settler might, however, decide against planting some crop, in which case he did not receive maximum credit. If he exceeded the crop allotment, he ran the risk of receiving no loans.

The seeds or cash loans assigned by the Department were granted to the village as a corporate unit: the village received the loaned capital and the village officers—the committee and the instructors—were responsible for its distribution. (The only exception to this centralized system was the electric supply; in most *moshavim* each home had its own meter, and each resident received a monthly bill.) None of the creditors dealt with individual settlers; the village was the responsible financial body.

Since marketing was also centralized—the settlers marketed their produce together—the village was presumably able to guarantee the return of the loans. Thus, following the harvest, the village officers received a check for the total amount of produce shipped to market. The loans previously extended were repaid, and only then were the profits divided among the producers.

The heart of this system was the bookkeeping office. Oren, like all *moshavim*, employed a bookkeeper who managed the villagers' accounts. Each settler had a file in the bookkeeper's ledger. The credits extended during the season were listed there: tractor costs, seed, fertilizer, insecticide, water, and so forth. In addition, the Department extended a monthly cash loan with which the settler made daily purchases: clothes, food, recreation, and so forth. Village taxes were also levied to meet the expense of various community services: the salaries of village secretary and bookkeeper, the weekly movie, a telephone, and so forth. The villagers also paid monthly dues to the settlement movement. Furthermore, there was a monthly payment for health services (Kupat Cholim, the largest national health plan, maintained a regional clinic in a nearby village) and for insurance premiums. These costs were all registered as debits. On the other side of the ledger the settlers' credits were entered: the value of goods shipped to market, the amount paid for guard duty, and the sums accredited for work in the village (public works undertaken during the winter or other community tasks performed). Profit or loss was thus easily computed: following the harvest, the settler was to receive the cash difference between credits and debits.

The accounting system—the costs of production and value of produce—is illustrated in the following three tables. The reproduced accounts are for the period between November, 1956 and November, 1957. They represent an average (Table 3), below-average (Table 4), and above-average (Table 5) farmer's balance sheet. M.D., of Table 3, is thirty-two and has a family of six children; he is responsible for operating the village's sprayer (see credit column). E.A., in Table 4, is a man approaching sixty, the father of eight children, most of whom work with him. D.L., the third man, is twenty-five and was recently married. He is a member of one of the large kinship groups and is probably the most successful farmer at Oren.

Several conclusions may be drawn from a comparison of these tables. The amount of water used by each of the three settlers was roughly equal. The quantity of fertilizer used, however, was very different; the amount listed in D.L.'s account is about

Table 3. Account of M.D. for period between November 1956
and November 1957

Debits			Credits		
Agricultural expenses			*Produce*		
1. Seeds and fertilizer	I£	441	1. Tomatoes	I£	973
2. Water		367	2. Garlic		92
3. Tractor		89	3. Potatoes (fall)		799
4. Spraying		87	4. Potatoes (spring)		95
	I£	984	5. Onions A		311
Village expenses			6. Onions B		105
1. Shepherd	I£	57	7. Peppers		21
2. Water clock		37		I£	2,396
3. Straw, etc.		142	*Village work*		
	I£	236	1. Spraying	I£	686
Other expenses			*Other income*		
1. Taxes	I£	254	1. Payments for		
2. Electricity		51	cotton damage *	I£	370
3. Guard duty		20			
4. Miscellaneous		90			
	I£	415			
Loans					
1. Monthly cash loans	I£	1,609			
Total	I£	3,244	Total	I£	3,452

* This records a payment made by the Department to each settler after the failure of the cotton crop. The Department agreed to pay the loss after the cotton seeds did not germinate.

twice that of E.A. To the extent that the proper use of fertilizers is related to success in farming, these differences help to explain D.L.'s success. As is also apparent, relatively large incomes may be acquired from village work; in E.A.'s case, village work amounted to roughly 30 per cent of his officially registered income. Most striking of all are the great differences in income: D.L.'s income far surpasses that of the other two villagers.

In theory, the accounts give a comprehensive view of the settlers' incomes. In reality, however, the credit side of the ledger was not all-inclusive, since it listed only the produce marketed

Table 4. Account of E.A. for period between November 1956 and November 1957

Debits			Credits		
Agricultural expenses			*Produce*		
1. Seeds and fertilizer	I£	267	1. Tomatoes	I£	690
2. Water		368	2. Garlic		91
3. Tractor		81	3. Potatoes (fall)		629
4. Spraying		71	4. Potatoes (spring)		269
	I£	787	5. Onions A		129
Village expenses			6. Onions B		135
1. Shepherd	I£	62		I£	1,943
2. Water gauge		37	*Village work*		
3. Straw		124	1. Paid work	I£	1,123
4. Work *		17	*Other income*		
	I£	240	1. Payments for		
Other expenses			cotton damage	I£	536
1. Taxes	I£	259	2. Insurance		200
2. Electricity		33	3. Miscellaneous		183
3. Guard duty		10		I£	919
4. Miscellaneous		99			
	I£	401			
Loans					
1. Monthly cash loans	I£	1,440			
Total	I£	2,868	Total	I£	3,985

* This is a payment shared by the villagers for special hired help (distributing seeds, produce boxes, etc.).

through official, village channels. A sizable proportion of the produce raised at Oren reached market by way of "illegal" channels and was not recorded in the bookkeeper's ledgers. How the "illegal" sales came to be—and the complications arising from them—requires additional explanation.

The *moshav's* cooperative credit system depends upon the controlled flow of goods to market. Oren's chief creditor was the Settlement Department: the Department provided the tractors and cash loans and also covered the village's debts to other institutions. (The financial relations between the Department and Ha'Mashbir or Mekorot were complicated; in what were largely "paper transactions" each might borrow hundreds of

Table 5. Account of D.L. for period between November, 1956 and November, 1957

Debits			Credits		
Agricultural expenses			*Produce*		
1. Seeds and fertilizer	I£	505	1. Tomatoes	I£	1,482
2. Water		345	2. Potatoes (fall)		1,241
3. Tractor		91	3. Potatoes (spring)		564
4. Spray		31	4. Onions A		740
	I£	972	5. Onions B		287
Village expenses			6. Peppers		33
1. Shepherd	I£	50		I£	4,347
2. Water gauge		37	*Village work*		
3. Straw		103	1. Paid work	I£	1,015
4. Work		131	*Other income*		
	I£	321	1. Payments for		
Other expenses			cotton damage	I£	679
1. Taxes	I£	226	2. Miscellaneous		30
2. Electricity		18		I£	709
3. Guard duty		19			
4. Miscellaneous		39			
	I£	302			
Loans					
1. Monthly cash loans	I£	2,951			
Total	I£	4,546	Total	I£	6,071

thousands of pounds from the other.) Consequently, the Department's financial stake in each settler's profit or loss was great. Only by control of the marketing of crops could the investment be guaranteed. In some cases, control was simple, since crops such as sugar beets or cotton had only one outlet: they were purchased by government agencies that owned the processing plants. Since the Department had close ties with these plants, the return of these funds was guaranteed. For this reason (as well as others) the Department often tended to increase the acreage of these industrial crops. It was more difficult, however, to control the marketing of vegetables. A settler or group of settlers might sell vegetables to a private merchant who paid them directly. In these instances, the settler simply pocketed the money without returning the credits previously extended. To cite another alternative, since Oren is located near Beersheba, some of the settlers marketed their produce privately in the town market. Many sent a portion of their produce through official channels, but marketed the other part privately.

A settler who chose "illegal" outlets saw his recorded debts grow, while at the same time he had a continuous, officially unrecorded income. Almost all of the settlers sold some crops in this fashion. At least a third of the villagers regularly marketed part of their produce privately, though usually in small amounts. (It is difficult to get accurate figures of "illegal" sales, but a good estimate is a weekly unrecorded income of between I £20 and I £40.) Marketing created a constant struggle between the village creditors—particularly the Settlement Department—and the settlers, and among the settlers themselves. It was one of the chief sources of tension.

The problems of credit control arose from various factors. In the first place, "beating the system" was an obvious lure: the possibility of receiving credits but not returning the loans had obvious attraction. A settler might rationalize his behavior by arguing that "the Department has so much money, it won't miss these few tomatoes." In such cases the Department might cut off credit to the settlers, but it was usually reluctant to do so. The settlers were its responsibility; how would they farm without credit? The settler who cheated could sometimes depend upon this attitude.

There were other reasons for illegal marketing. While the settlers were guaranteed a minimum price for their produce, the price paid was often substantially below the actual market price. If the settler could receive a better price, he usually turned to private, illegal channels. Moreover, if the settlers did not receive their monthly loans from the Department as promised—a situation that often occurred—they resorted to illegal means. Apart from these reasons, many settlers simply did not understand the intricacies of the credit system. How it was that credits were fixed to one's account in a bookkeeping system, and then much later subtracted from the value of produce, was often not comprehended. Since there was inevitably a long gap—sometimes extending for several months—between marketing and receiving payment, many settlers were unaware of their real financial condition. When their profits finally did appear in the bookkeeper's report, they were convinced that somewhere there had been an error or that someone had taken their just rewards. Rather than rely upon a system they did not fully understand, they chose to act in a more traditional, direct fashion.

Cooperative marketing imposed tensions among the settlers themselves. Loans and credits, it will be recalled, were extended to the village as a whole. For example, the village paid a lump sum to Mekorot for all the water used by the villagers; there was then an internal division of costs, as each settler's account was debited according to the amount of water he used. The sole source of village finances were the crops, plus the public works provided by the Department. However, not all settlers shipped equal amounts of produce; those who were successful shipped more, and those who failed shipped little. Some, as we just saw, marketed their goods privately and did not contribute to the sums available for community payment of debts. The result of this arrangement was that the successful producers in effect paid the costs of the less successful. This was not a payment made by choice, but rather one that arose from the nature of the system. Since all credits and profits were centralized, those who contributed more were forced to bear a heavier burden of the debts of the entire community. In many instances, the successful producers did not receive their full profits, because the produce they shipped was used to cover the total village debt. This situation sometimes led the larger producers to sell their crops privately, since they were then assured of receiving payment.

Cooperative farming—the heart of the *moshav* system—was thus only partially realized at Oren. Not only was the community itself artificial, the productive system was imposed and had little resemblance to the settlers' past experiences. The demands of this system, as well as its internal failures, led to recurring community crises. As we shall see shortly, these strains divided the community into different interest groups and consequently were important factors in the development of new social alignments.

The Moshav *and the System of Settlement*

The description of Oren up to this point has emphasized the settlers. Oren's social system, however, included not only the new immigrants, but also the various institutions that served the village. Most prominent among these was the Settlement Department; much of what daily transpired at Oren depended upon Department plans and personnel.

A settler who joined Oren received from the Settlement Department a home and plot of land under irrigation, various agricultural tools, a milch cow, and the use of a horse and cart. (A horse and cart were given to every two settlers.) The Department also made yearly investment grants in the form of additional pipe, implements, and new production systems (for example, chicken raising was recently introduced at Oren); there were, in addition, other occasional capital grants. While the settlers used this equipment, the house and the tools legally remained the property of the Department. When a settler joined a *moshav* he signed a contract guaranteeing to return all the equipment in good condition in the event that he left the village. A settler could not legally buy or sell a house in the village, rent the land to another, or sell the equipment; if he sold or rented he was liable to be prosecuted. However, as long as he remained in the village, the home and equipment were his to use.[1]

The Department was responsible for planning and directing each villager's agricultural work. Agricultural and community planning advanced at several levels: there were national, regional, and village programs. To begin with, national planning was conceived and developed in Department offices in Jerusalem. Programs were then transmitted to the administrative districts (the *chevel*). The country as a whole was divided into five districts: Chevel Ha'Negev, Chevel Lachish (between Nir Am–Beth Kama and Kastina), Chevel Ha'Har (the Jerusalem area and the northern hill settlements), Chevel Ha'Tichon (Chedera–Rechovot) and Chevel Ha'Tzafon (the area between Chedera and Naharia). Each district was then subdivided into regions (*azorim*); there were, for example, three regions in the Negev district. Each region was in turn responsible for a number of settlements; Oren thus belonged to the Beersheba region.

Each of these administrative units within the Department employed a series of officials: there were "chief instructors," who worked on a national level, "district instructors," who operated

---

[1] When and at what rate the funds loaned to the villagers would be repaid was never clarified. According to contract, the funds disbursed by public agencies for housing, irrigation systems, village stores, etc., were to be repaid, and some of the veteran *moshavim* and *kibbutzim* have already completed repayment. Whether or not the new immigrants would be required to return these loans was a moot question.

on a *chevel*-wide basis, "regional instructors," who served a particular region, and "village instructors," attached to each new
moshav. Direction and planning thus moved through a series of
steps: from central offices in Jerusalem to district headquarters
in Beersheba, from there to regional offices, and, finally, out into
each *moshav*.

Agency experts on the various levels drew up farming plans
and financial budgets. The planting schedules were first drafted
on a national scale and then divided between districts. Quotas
were also set for each village. Capital was similarly allocated;
depending upon available resources (this meant primarily the
amount of money raised by various financial campaigns outside
of Israel), appropriations were made to the district and to the
various villages. This money was used to purchase capital goods
(tractors for the tractor stations or pipe for the settlers' fields).
Funds for monthly loans were also allotted to the district, which
then granted loans to the villages.

The most sensitive point within this complex structure was
the individual *moshav*. While the structure as a whole was built
to serve the settlers, only the village instructors were regularly
in contact with the Department's "clients." The behavior of the
village *madrich* was therefore decisive in many ways.

The corps of instructors in a new immigrant village usually
consisted of two agricultural experts, a management or "communal" instructor, and an instructress for women. Most instructors were quite young; in 1957 the farm manager at Oren was
aged twenty-four, and the two farm experts, twenty-seven and
thirty-four. The manager was married and had an infant, and
one of the farm experts was also married. The training they received prior to undertaking their jobs was modest. The farm
manager had left a *kibbutz* six months before going to Oren; he
had no formal training in community management, though he
later attended a two-month Department-sponsored course for
farm managers. One of the agricultural instructors was an Is-

raeli, born and reared in an older farming community. The second expert had immigrated to Israel in 1947 as a member of an *aliyat noar* group and received agricultural training in one of the older *moshavim*. Both agricultural instructors occasionally attended brief courses in crop management. Instructors usually spent one or two years—sometimes much less—in a village; between 1955 and 1962 there was a rotation of four farm managers and eight farm instructors at Oren.

The tasks of an agricultural instructor were relatively well-defined: he supervised the farming process and was responsible for guiding the settlers in their new work. The agricultural instructor directly controlled the mechanized farm work: he supervised the tractors, the spraying, the mechanical seeding, and so forth. Several times a week he toured the settlers' fields and advised them regarding the progress of their work. The instructor might suggest that the settler had irrigated too much or too little, that he had neglected weeding his plants, or that his tomatoes were not properly tied; depending upon his relationship with the settler, he might offer to help or restrict himself to verbal comments. While he controlled the planning process, the instructor depended upon the settler to carry out the plans. In many instances, it was precisely here that the imponderables of crop management entered. For if the settler did not irrigate properly, or if he allowed the weeds to grow, his yields and profits—and the entire complex structure—were affected.

Nevertheless, the instructor could exert direct pressure upon the settler to tend his land. His most effective weapon was control of the credit system. It will be recalled that the Department extended a monthly loan to each settler. While different methods were attempted, a typical procedure was to vary the amount of the loan depending upon the condition of each settler's crops. The instructor checked each plot and submitted a report describing its condition. A person whose crops promised a good yield—one who had presumably tended his fields well—received a larger loan than a man who worked less diligently. (The loans received by D.L. recorded on Table 5 are about twice those of the other two settlers.) Since few settlers had a continuous supply of money apart from these loans, this was a powerful work incentive. Armed with this weapon, the instructor prodded the settlers into working.

The *moshav* system of marketing, credits, loans, and mechanization was intricate and complex. The responsibility for arranging the many facets of organized village life belonged to the farm manager. This instructor represented the village before various national and regional agencies. But his main responsibility was in directing the community's financial structure. Together with the elected village representatives—the secretary and committee—he discussed and determined village policy.

How a farm manager handled his tasks may best be illustrated by outlining an incident typical of village life. The events sketched below indicate the relation of the instructor—and the settlement system as a whole—to the farming process. How the system worked (or failed to work) and the positions taken by the various people within it will be indicated.

A spring planting schedule called for, among other crops, the sowing of a *dunam* of onions. The villagers were told that if they planted onions and the crop succeeded, they would receive a guaranteed price for their produce. Although they had never before raised onions, they agreed to the plan; the promised price was quite high and nearly everyone planted the crop. The seeds were provided by an affiliate of the settlement movement to which Oren belonged; at that period in the community's development, farm planning was managed by this group and not directly by the Settlement Department. Later, after the crop had been planted, responsibility was transferred to the Department.

The settlers planted, irrigated, and cultivated the crop. They followed the instructors' advice, and in most cases the crop seemed promising. The farm manager then asked the regional

representative of the marketing cooperative, Tnuva, to inspect
the crop so that it might be sent to market. The official arrived,
walked through the fields, and agreed that the onions were in
good condition. He suggested, however, that they not be harvested yet, since there was then a glut of onions on the market;
if they were left in the ground, they would dry out and fetch a
better price. The instructor agreed and informed the settlers of
the new plan: the onions were not to be harvested yet but would
later be sold half dried. The settlers continued to care for the
onions. Several weeks later, the manager again asked the market
representative to inspect the crop; this he did and agreed to their
promise, but he urged that the onions still not be sent to market.
The instructor reluctantly agreed but told the Tnuva official
that soon they would have to ship the onions, since they were
growing larger and would soon be unmarketable. Again the instructor told the settlers of the plan, and they, though uneasy,
agreed.

A week later, the instructor contacted the Tnuva agent and
asked that the onions be shipped to market. The Tnuva official
this time agreed, although he was skeptical of the price the
onions would fetch. The instructor told the settlers to harvest
the crop and ordered a truck to load the produce. The onions
were picked, the truck arrived, and the produce proceeded to
market. Three days later, the instructor asked that more onions
be shipped and ordered several trucks. That morning, however,
only one truck arrived to pick up the produce, and only a part
of the crop was shipped. Most of the onions remained in the
shed. The instructor telephoned the trucking agency and asked
why more trucks had not been sent. The trucking official answered that the Tnuva officers had instructed him to send only
one truck and that he had complied with this order. Disturbed,
the instructor went to the Tnuva regional office in Beersheba the
next day. The Tnuva official then related the following information: the onions shipped by Oren were too large; there were bet-

ter onions on the market, and Oren's onions were, in comparison, too large to be sold. The Tnuva representative had received
orders not to accept onions of that size. The representative was
sorry, he understood the problem, but such were his orders, and
he could do nothing.

Upon hearing this information the manager was enraged. He
had twice been asked to keep the onions from the market; since
these instructions had been followed, the onions were naturally
larger and now they were unacceptable! What would he do
with them? Tnuva was, according to tradition and by contract,
responsible for receiving all the village's crops; yet now they
would not accept them. The manager then went to the Settlement Department offices and told his superiors of the situation.
They too were disturbed. They had extended loans to the settlers against these crops; what would happen to their investment? These higher echelon officials contacted the Tnuva
personnel. They were given the same information: Oren's
onions were too large, and they would not be accepted. The
Department officials promised to discuss the matter further with
the Tnuva executives, and they also asked the instructor to bring
pressure to bear upon Tnuva.

While the officials attempted to arrange some agreement, the
onions remained in the ground or rotted in the central shed. The
settlers, of course, were deeply distressed: after all their work,
was their produce simply to rot, and were they themselves to
sink deeper into debt? They protested to the manager, to the village officials, and to the Department. Their complaints were
repeated and bitter, and the responsible officials, both in and outside the village, could only assent and reassure them that the
issue was "being looked into."

The Department executives continued to seek some solution.
Oren's farm manager turned to the settlement movement to
which Oren was affiliated and asked that they, too, put pressure
upon Tnuva. The complexity of the situation was only then re-

vealed. As it turned out, Tnuva had been told not to accept the onions by order of a higher authority! The national government board, which set guaranteed vegetable prices and paid subsidies on them, had requested Tnuva not to accept these large onions. There was a glut on the market, and the board was paying thousands of pounds in subsidies for onions that were being dumped and burned. The marketing board further claimed that the onions had not been planted according to instructions, that the seeds originally provided were not the specified variety, and that it consequently would not be responsible for what happened to the crop.

The struggle then focused upon the marketing board: the settlement movement and the Department brought pressure to bear so that the onions would be accepted. At one point, the farm manager threatened to bring the settlers with their onions to the Tnuva central warehouse in Tel Aviv and stage a "demonstration," but the settlers themselves vetoed this plan. Although they were agitated, they took the position that it was essentially the Department's problem. They had been told to plant onions, and they had; now that plans had gone awry, it was the Department's worry, not theirs. Besides, who would listen to them?

Negotiations continued for several more days. Finally, after weeks of bickering, an agreement was reached. The Department executives in Beersheba announced that the onions would be accepted and a price paid for them which was close to the promised price. This arrangement was essentially an agreement in which the Department forfeited all its claims to the produce—it took the loss—and the settlers received an almost token sum; since the settlers' investment was cancelled (the Department cancelled part of its tractor, water, seed, and fertilizer bill), a slight profit was realized. The onions were duly placed on trucks, taken out of the village, and dumped: the "onion saga" was finished.

This incident illustrates various facets of the settlement system. The role of the farm manager was well represented in these events. Coordinating the various threads in the system was the *madrich*'s responsibility: in this instance he announced the farm schedule, ordered trucks for the produce, negotiated with the Tnuva representative, and, when plans went awry, sought to bring pressure to bear upon Tnuva, the Department, the settlement movement, and the marketing board. In determining policies the manager consulted with two different groups, his superiors in the Department and the elected village officials. Within the Department, the instructor's authority was limited; he administered rather than decided policy. In the village, however, his status was considerable and his influence great. He met regularly with the village committee, at which times plans were discussed and decisions made. Generally speaking, the manager's comments were decisive. After all, he knew the Israeli world much better than the settlers. While the manager was ostensibly a teacher, preparing the settlers for their future role of self-management, he tended to dominate planning and decision-making. His sources of information were much better than those of the settlers. In many instances he did not transmit this knowledge but rather made his own decisions. This was particularly true in regard to financial matters. Oren's debts and payments were exceedingly complex, and the instructor tended to manage them without consulting the settlers. Thus, for example, when one manager left Oren and another replaced him, the new instructor and the settlers suddenly found that the village had contracted debts nobody was aware of.

Being part of two systems—the Department and the village —a manager was faced with conflicting pressures. As a Department worker he knew that the flow of goods to market had to be controlled, or else the loan structure would collapse and the Department fail to receive the credits it had extended. Yet, living within the village and knowing the settlers' problems, he might tacitly permit the settlers to market their goods privately. Sometimes a manager was removed from a village because he no longer successfully represented the Department's interest; he felt the pressures and sentiments of the settlers themselves too strongly.

The roles played by the various members of the settlement system were also illustrated in the incident described above. Department executives on the regional and district levels played an important part in the negotiations. These personnel sought to solve the problems of their "constitutents." Each region or district always attempted to secure better services and more capital for its villages. The districts themselves competed: each tried to secure the best personnel, larger planting schedules, more water, and so forth. When, to cite one example, a sugar beet processing factory was to be built in the south, the Negev district competed with a neighboring district to secure the factory for its own area. These decisions were ultimately made on a higher level, in Jerusalem or Tel Aviv. There the various executives played a continuous game of internal politics. The director, sub-director, and other top district executives often spent days with marketing boards, national water authorities, and government ministries, as they bickered for larger quotas, more capital, different credit systems, and so forth. They might use various strategies in their competition; in certain situations the director of a district might turn to a political party for aid, or he might use the press as a means of mobilizing opinion. (This latter tactic was usually reserved for extreme situations; most often the allied agencies attempted to settle their differences privately, without public appeals.)

In the case related, the farm manager turned for support to the settlement movement to which Oren was affiliated. There were two major movements: one represented the religious political parties, the other, the dominant secular labor party. Both movements were organized and led by members of the older, pre-State *moshavim;* while the number of immigrant *moshavim* far outnumbered the pre-State settlements, the movements were dominated by older settlers. These federations were, in effect, pressure groups: they represented the settlers' interests before the various planning boards and authorities. Since the movements' agents were older settlers intimately acquainted with the elite power groups, their lobbying was often effective.

The settlement movements and the Department tended to work cooperatively. Each movement's representatives met with the Department executives; both groups jointly sought to influence higher level officials. There was formally a division of labor between the two: the Department's mandate extended to technical agricultural development, while the movement was to care for social problems and internal political issues. This division was obviously artificial, however: under the conditions of an immigrant *moshav*, growing tomatoes was often a social problem, and feuds between kinship groups might affect sugar beet production. In effect, both groups dealt with the same kinds of problems and often with identical situations. This often resulted in tension between the Department and the movements: there were failures in communication, differences in approach, different plans or tactics.

There were also ideological differences between the Department and the settlement movements. The Department was primarily concerned with completing a task: it wished to turn immigrants into productive farmers. It had a natural interest in efficiency, in getting its job done well. It was not, for the most part, ideologically committed to the *moshav* as a system; if the settlers might be more efficient producers within a different framework, the Department seemed prepared to introduce changes in the *moshav* system. The movements, on the other hand, were ideologically committed to the *moshav: moshav* ideals had a more permanent value for them. The movements tended to be conservative, the Department more flexible and experimental.

What is most striking about the incident related above, how-ever, is not the activities of the different bureaucracies or the intrabureaucratic tensions, but rather the dependent pose of the settlers. While they were the basic element in the entire structure—the venture was conceived and developed in their behalf—the villagers had only limited control over community affairs. If and to what extent their agricultural labor was to be rewarded depended not only upon their diligence, but also upon the success of the Department managers. It is certainly clear that failures in farming resulted both from the settlers' inefficiency and from managerial error and mismanagement.

The impact of this system was very great. Central planning and control, in which the settlers did not participate and regard-ing which they had only limited information, made them highly dependent; they reacted to situations rather than controlling events themselves. Passivity of a kind, as well as "illegal acts" or sabotage, were products of this relationship. When central plan-ning failed, it is hardly surprising that everyone clamored for increased financial protection, and that some marketed their produce privately. The system therefore favored—indeed, rein-forced—the settlers' passivity and dependence. It was only later, when the planting and credit arrangements were modified, that the settlers became more active and autonomous. However, these developments, as described in the final chapter, must await a closer analysis of the village's internal political and administra-tive systems. To these issues we turn next.

CHAPTER V

People and Power:
Social Alignments
and Community Control

OREN'S development traces the growth of a new community. When first formed, the community was entirely artificial; in a brief period, however, its composition and social structure changed. These changes came about both as a consequence of migrations and as a result of the village's form of organization. The network of relations between villagers was based upon personal ties, but allegiances shifted according to the external pressures facing the community. How and why these allegiances shifted, and, in particular, the relationship between social units and political formations, is the main topic of this chapter.

An analysis of social roles and relations at Oren begins in the family. The family was the basic residence and economic unit: a man and his wife and children lived together and shared with one another their love and labor. So long as he was active, the father wielded authority: he decided when to work and who must work, controlled the family purse, and determined what would be bought and for whom. His decisions were normally final; if he asked that more wine be purchased or that his children work rather than attend school, his word carried great weight. If challenged, he might threaten and sometimes impose physical punishment.

Although most wives followed their husband's wishes, they were not without influence. Men made decisions, but they usually consulted their wives. Even if he did not seek her views, a wife could press her opinions upon her husband. Women's nagging was often effective; at every opportunity she voiced or insinuated her feelings. A woman had even more powerful weapons: she might cook badly, leave the house and children unmanaged, or refuse to sleep with her husband. If he beat her, she might run away or appeal to her family for help.

Children were desired, and families were usually large; Western birth control techniques, while vaguely understood, were not followed. Parent-child relations were typically warm. The school-age children tended, at least outwardly, to be submissive; they responded quickly to their parents' direction. As the children grew older, however, relationships with their parents often became strained. The boys in particular assumed greater responsibility, often becoming the main worker in the family's fields. The father still controlled the purse, however, and continued to dole out money. This financial dependence was often a source of frustration and tension.

Relations between the generations were also strained by the youngsters' greater understanding of the Israeli scene. Schools, youth groups, and the army were among the institutions that introduced the young to the new patterns of Israeli culture. Insofar as these patterns were successfully mastered, the new knowledge lent the youngsters additional influence. School or army-educated young people understood the language and meanings of the *moshav* world far better than their parents; they were also better equipped to arrange affairs in the outer world of bureaucracies. As their skill increased, so too did their importance; they were increasingly depended upon. Since many fathers were unwilling to relinquish authority, family tensions often developed. The conflict between generations, which was already evident in Morocco, was intensified in the *moshav:* an older social crisis was renewed and given added dimensions.

Three different types of family systems may be identified in the *moshav:* isolated family units, extended families, and kinship groups. An isolated family unit had no other relatives in the village. It stood structurally by itself, without ties to other family groups. There were eight isolated families at Oren. Generally speaking, these family units did not maintain regular cooperative activities with others. They had no inherent means of support —in order to be effective, they had either to support one of the kin groups or form an independent group. Moreover, isolated families felt no inclusive attachments—they were part of no larger system. Village social controls often did not include them; such families did not imagine themselves bound to the *moshav* as a social unit or to their neighbors as individuals. As a consequence, they tended to flaunt *moshav* rules and decisions. Many of the settlers who sold their produce privately in the market at Beersheba were of this family type.

Only one extended family, consisting of a father and his three married sons, was present in the village. Each of the sons had a separate home, and each functioned as a separate economic unit. Limited cooperation was maintained between the father and his sons, but the brothers maintained only routine contact. Since the elder father often pressed his authority—an attitude that the sons were not always ready to comply with—relations between father and sons, and between brothers, were strained. This bloc of families was therefore never able to achieve the degree of internal cooperation necessary to become an important force in the village.

At Oren, as in many other immigrant *moshavim,* the village was dominated by clusters of kin. These groups varied in size between small groups composed of several brothers-in-law or brothers, and the two larger kin groups. Within the smaller kin groups, the relations between members fluctuated; in some circumstances they cooperated with one another (participating in cooperative harvesting, for example), in other situations they acted individually. In most political issues, however, kinsmen drew together, supporting each other's position. The influence of these smaller groups was limited by their size, and they did not have a large following. On the other hand, the two larger kin groups were extremely powerful; they became the village's major sociopolitical groups.

These two large groups were differently organized. One of them, composed of the Levi and Paro families, included two groups of cousins. There were five Levi families: the elder uncle, his two nephews, and his two sons-in-law. The Paros were the Levi's maternal cousins and included three brothers and their two maternal cousins. Each group individually constituted a cooperative economic unit: the Levis worked together and so did the Paros, and in certain occasions they all pooled their labor. Within this cluster, the closest ties were between the Levi families: the uncle and his two nephews worked their land entirely in common and established a joint fund from which they made large capital purchases.

Leadership within the Levi-Paro group was divided between the elder uncle, Yaacov, and his older nephew, Shimon. Yaacov, the village rabbi, was influential both within the family and in the village as a whole. In the family, his opinions were followed in regard to ceremonial and religious issues; his opinions regarding farm problems were respected, but less decisive. In village politics, however, Yaacov's point of view was important. His role within the kin group was symbolized by the location of his house: all of the Levis lived in houses that had formerly been the homes of instructors, and Yaacov's home was the first in the row. He was a powerful and often final authority.

Age traditionally drew respect and deference; in Morocco the eldest sibling tended to assume leadership. Shimon, the older brother, was a key figure within this kin group. Ambitious and aggressive, Shimon was influential in village affairs. He and Chaim, his younger brother, sometimes quarreled, at times rather violently; Chaim was closer to the instructors and represented a more progressive point of view. There were thus tensions among kin, but whenever conflicts arose, the group inevitably united.

The Levis were successful farmers: they worked long and diligently, had mastered the techniques, and profited from their labor. They knew Hebrew well and were among the few settlers who read Hebrew newspapers. One of the Levi's was the first settler to own a horse (soon thereafter many others purchased horses), and later, the families jointly purchased a tractor. Agriculturally, the Levis were the pace setters. Their cousins, the Paros, accepted their leadership. Generally speaking, this group supported a "hard line" in village politics: since they themselves were successful producers, they put pressure upon the less successful so that the full brunt of village costs would not fall upon them alone.

The second of the two large kin groups at Oren, the Dehan families, was more of a loose confederation than a tight bloc. As a group, they included fourteen families: two brothers, two brothers-in-law, and ten maternal and paternal cousins. Several of the cousins were, at best, distant relatives; they were from the same town in Morocco, and their "kinship" was more a matter of convenience and politics than of blood or marriage. Most of the Dehans lived near one another, along one street. At certain times, the kinsmen cooperated with each other, but usually they worked independently. In the evenings the families gathered to-

gether in one of the houses, discussing village affairs over innumerable cups of tea. The women were particularly close and
often exchanged help and favors.

Several members of the Dehan families were among the successful farmers. The acknowledged leader among them was
Moshe, the eldest cousin. Ambitious and yet rather permissive,
Moshe had early learned to read and write Hebrew. Soon after
arriving at Oren, he became active in community affairs, and
later he served as the village secretary. With the backing of his
families, and with the support of other settlers, Moshe represented an alternative to the leadership of the Levis, and to
Shimon Levi in particular. A popular figure within the village,
his political talents made him influential. Within the family and
in the village, Moshe usually operated by consultation; he spent
long hours in discussion before seeking to implement some
policy.

These larger kin groups had many advantages. By their sheer
size, they were able to dominate village policies, and they therefore became the main political units. Moreover, they had "built-
in" systems of cooperation; aid and assistance was easily exchanged between kinsmen. In addition, they never felt isolated;
they could always fall back upon one another. This latter fact is
particularly important when seen in the perspective of their new
life in Oren: the kin group represented a known social field in an
otherwise new social universe. Its members felt participation
within the group. They even generated an *élan:* they were
"Dehans" or "Levis," and effective social control was usually
maintained within the group.

While kinship was the basic principle of social organization,
other factors also tended to join persons together. Principal
among these was friendship; personal attraction or conviviality
led to visiting and, at times, to limited cooperation. Several
friendship groups developed between persons from the same

Moroccan area. While previously they may have been only acquaintances, in the strangeness of the *moshav* they struck up
closer relations. Friendship groups sometimes grew into minor
cliques, as the various members supported each other's ambitions. Usually, however, these were only temporary groups;
joint farming efforts were rarely sustained, since the group
lacked firm leadership and sufficient common interest. The members quarreled, and the group dissolved. Friendship groups
could become effective only by supporting a major kin unit.
With power split between the two groups of kin, the friendship
groups were sometimes able to practice effective politics. Although this added to their individual influence, it diminished the
group's effectiveness: they remained temporary, shifting cliques,
appendages to the larger units.

To some extent, age was also a principle of social cohesion.
This was especially true of the younger married men and of the
bachelors. The young men—particularly those who had been in
aliyat noar groups or in the army—discovered that they had
much in common. In contrast with others, they knew the country and the language. The young men often visited with each
other, sometimes traveling together to various national events.
Since they were among the better farmers, they were respected
village members. Their influence as a group was limited, however, by their members' affiliations with other social units. Several
were politically independent and stood apart from the warring
factions. On the other hand, those young men who were members
of politically active families tended to support their kin. Ties
based upon age were unable to withstand family bonds; the latter
were too powerful to resist.

The bachelors were still another potential social group. Bachelors were boys who had not yet served in the army, older boys
living at home with their parents. Bored with village life and
at odds with their parents, they sought each other's com-

pany. After work they sat together near the general store, drinking beer and swapping tales. Some evenings they would play cards or listen to the radio, and at times they made sporadic efforts to organize dancing or to play soccer. Most ultimately left the community. Within the village they were an amorphous, ineffectual element; influence was barred to them by their indefinite ties and was reserved for the married men, the "permanent" residents.

In addition to these social units—the groups based upon kinship, friendship, and age—another social group was present: the instructors. In a general way, a *madrich*'s social ties were mainly outside the village. That is, his circle of friends rarely included the villagers; if it did, however, they were the most atypical villagers, the ones who were most like the instructors. These were the young men, particularly those who had spent several years in the army or at an Israeli school. Depending upon the instructor's ability to mix freely with the immigrants, the relations might be pleasing; they were often strained, however, since neither party was fully at ease with the other.

An instructor might sometimes enter into warm relations with an older settler. This relationship was bound to engender prestige: the instructor, the symbol of the new life and the dispenser of things desired, lent status to whomever he became friendly with. He was thus able to support a group or plan indirectly. While instructors might use their prestige in this way, they had to do it carefully; if their contacts were limited to only a few settlers—if some were obviously closer to them than others— they ran the risk of becoming a partisan of one group and were likely to be accused of favoritism. Their friendships therefore needed to be carefully calculated.

Social solidarity in the village was expressed in a variety of ways: men sometimes worked together, visited one another, and some supported each other in village affairs. This latter activity was most significant of all. Village politics—the struggle for influence and power—cannot be understood without reference to the village's social structure. At Oren, kinship and influence were firmly intertwined.

It will be recalled that shortly after the Moroccan group reached Oren they were introduced to the new political system: elections were then held for a committee (in Hebrew, *vaad*) and secretary. From the beginning of their careers as *moshav* members, each settler hoped to assume some position within this formal political structure. Everyone wanted to be a committee member, and there were numerous candidates for secretary. There are various reasons for this interest. Membership on the committee was a symbol of prestige; to be elected to the *vaad* increased one's status. More important, it gave considerable material advantage. Members were "on the inside": they were the first to receive information that only later became public. This was obviously advantageous. (For this reason, it was always difficult to keep meetings private: the other settlers often tried to enter or listened to the proceedings through closed doors and windows.) Most important of all, the committee was empowered to make decisions: together with the instructor, the committee allocated houses, appointed community personnel, and decided who would get what and in what order. In the course of a few years, hundreds of thousands of pounds and invaluable equipment were channeled through this group. Committee membership was therefore a precious asset.

Since election to the committee was determined by democratic procedure, the path to membership was clear: one needed the support of others. Given the social structure of the village, the large kinship groups had an obvious advantage: kinsmen inevitably supported one another. The two large kinship groups therefore controlled the political system. As a result, at various times one of the kin groups dominated the committee to the exclusion of the other, or some *modus vivendi* was entered into by the two groups and both shared control.

The struggle for power thus became a contest between the Levis and the Dehans. Since neither group was numerically large enough to constitute an absolute majority, continuous political contests ensued: each bloc enlisted and found supporters from among the "unaffiliated." Factions, or political groups which contested for control of the village, were thereby formed. Membership in a faction was based upon various factors: personal friendships, old hates and quarrels, or a more objective belief in the greater skill or wisdom of one group or the other. Of course, once in power the kin groups, the faction's core unit, were obligated to represent the interests of their supporters. Those in power faced the dilemma of all policy-makers: if their decisions were contrary to the interests of their adherents, they faced the danger of losing support. The Dehan families could usually count on the votes of ten to fifteen other villagers, thereby increasing the faction's strength to twenty-nine families. Their opponents, the Levi faction, included—in addition to the ten members of the kinship group—another eight to ten supporters. The Dehan's therefore had the advantage of size.

The seemingly unending series of village crises placed effective issues in the hands of the two factions. Each crisis lent opportunities for one group to accuse the other of mismanagement and then to seek to unseat it. The newness of village life, the extreme dependence of the *moshav*, and the farming system all contributed to a condition of political instability and change. The term of office of a committee was often short, as new crises and rising discontent led to new elections.

The village political system may perhaps best be seen by outlining the development of a single incident. Typical of a repeated series of events, it well illustrates many of the factors thus far discussed.

Following a long series of conflicts climaxed by a wild fist fight, the leadership of the Levi families had been repudiated. The entire village rose against them in a rare and short-lived

show of unity. A new committee was elected, this time controlled by the Dehan families. For several months following the
election, relations between the Levis and the other settlers were
quiet but smoldering; the Levis did not come to meetings, they
were not invited to weddings, and so forth. Later, however,
they began attending community meetings again. Moreover,
they began to agitate against the rule of the Dehan families.
Some of the "discontents"—those failing in agriculture—began
to cluster about them.

One of the members of the new committee was a young and
energetic boy, Masoud. Masoud had come from Morocco with
an *aliyat noar* group and had spent three years in an agricultural
school; he was a successful farmer and probably the most acculturated among the Moroccan settlers. Masoud was a close friend
of the instructors (prior to his marriage he had roomed with
them) and despite his youth, he was also a respected man in the
village. He had held a variety of positions in the community and
was at the time responsible for the shipment of crops to market.
He received and weighed the produce, and later sent slips with
the amounts to the village bookkeeper, who registered these figures in the shipper's account.

One evening Yaacov Calah came to Masoud and complained
that an error had been made in registering the amount of
produce he had shipped; Yaacov claimed that he had shipped
more than Masoud had recorded. Masoud was at first uncon-
cerned by the accusation, since such complaints were common.
He told Yaacov that he would check the accounts, and that perhaps he, Masoud, had erred. Yaacov, however, became agitated.
The thought that he had been growing crops, working long and
hard, and in the end had not been credited with the full harvest,
made him increasingly angry. Soon he was shouting at Masoud,
accusing him of being a thief; he screamed that he would bring
the issue before the entire community on Saturday in the synagogue.

Masoud himself was by then upset. The next day he checked his accounts and discovered that an error had in fact been made; he notified the bookkeeper and then told Yaacov Calah. Masoud imagined that Yaacov would be mollified, but he was not. On the contrary, he was convinced more than ever that Masoud had been stealing from him. Had his accusation not forced Masoud to say that he had made a mistake? What if he had not complained? What of all the crops he had shipped before? He again accused Masoud of theft and promised to raise the issue in the synagogue.

On Saturday morning, before the reading of the Bible, Yaacov stood up in the synagogue and accused Masoud of having stolen produce from him; Masoud undervalued the produce Yaacov had shipped and then credited the difference to his own account. The accusation caused something of a sensation. Masoud chose not to come to the synagogue, but he was defended by his father and uncle. The Dehan families also sided with Masoud; they were skeptical of the accusation. It was simply a mistake, they said. On the other side, Yaacov Calah's brother and nephews came to his support; they began to insinuate that this theft was common practice and that it was by theft rather than by dint of hard work that Masoud had prospered. This was followed by a violent attack in the same vein by a neighbor of Masoud's father, a man who had a long history of quarrels with the father. By this time, the proceedings were becoming more stormy. The Levis had remained silent throughout. Finally, they suggested that a general meeting be held that evening and that the issue be discussed and some decision made. Everyone agreed, and the synagogue service continued. During the rest of the day, however, small knots of men gathered and discussed the issue. The Dehan families visited the instructor (the instructors never attended the synagogue) and told him what had happened. The instructor expressed surprise at the accusation but promised that he would attend the meeting.

The meeting was held in the evening before the weekly movie. Moshe Dehan, the secretary, chaired the proceedings. Yaacov Calah began by repeating his accusations; since he spoke in Arabic, the instructor asked that his words be translated. The translation was lost, however, in the general uproar. The partisans on both sides began to scream at one another, Masoud's family and friends shouting back at the Calah families. Whoever had grudges against the "accused" and his family joined in the attack. In the midst of the confusion the instructor jumped up and attempted to restore order. When it was quiet enough for him to be heard, he asked Yaacov Calah if he was really convinced that there had been a theft; if there had been, he said, the police should be called immediately. He asked if Yaacov was willing to sign a complaint. Yaacov was taken aback by this formal attack; he stammered, hampered as much by the Hebrew as by the situation. One of his nephews called out that he was willing to file a complaint. By then, however, the steam had gone out of the attack; besides, the movie was about to begin. The instructor again asked, in a disbelieving tone, if someone were willing to press formal charges. No one replied. Masoud had sat silently throughout; his only comment had been at the outset of the meeting, when he asked that he be replaced as produce receiver. But the instructor requested that he not resign, since there was no one in the village who could perform the job as well. The instructor also suggested that the committee be enlarged: he proposed that Chaim Levi and Machlouf Dehan be co-opted to the committee. Although membership is legally determined by democratic election, no one opposed the suggestion. Chaim was the least objectionable of the Levis from the Dehan point of view, and he was generally respected throughout the village. Everyone then filed out to attend the movie, though the two families involved in the dispute—the Calahs' and Masoud's kin—continued to quarrel, reviving old issues.

The Levis had again sat quietly throughout the meeting; they had never liked Masoud, but they did not find the issue easily exploitable. Besides, they now had a representative on the committee. Their ambitions were not stilled, however; during the next week they gathered with the "discontents" and the Calah families, speaking against the committee and its policies.

The next chance for the Levis to regain control came rather quickly, and again it involved Masoud. Masoud had been responsible for loading sugar beets on trucks during the beet harvest. He had not yet been paid for his work, since there were no funds for paying him, and the village, as usual, had little money. An opportunity for settling the account offered itself with the onion harvest. Oren's onions, it will be recalled, had not been shipped because of a glut on the market; the Settlement Department agreed to pay the costs, and the onions were dumped and burned. The actual dumping had been assigned to a truck driver in a local trucking cooperative; he was to pick up the onions, estimate their weight, and then burn them. Since the price paid for the onions was low, one of the instructors conceived the idea of arranging with the driver to overestimate the weight. The driver agreed to this arrangement, and since there was no real check on the figures, a higher estimate was submitted to the department.

The only persons in the village who were aware of this arrangement were the instructor, Masoud, and the secretary. The instructor planned to use the money (if the Department would agree to pay the higher amount) for some public use. But Masoud asked if this money might not be used to repay his work in the sugar beet harvest. This seemed reasonable to the instructor, who decided to enlarge the amount of onions in Masoud's account from two to four and a half tons; this extra sum would pay back his services.

Masoud duly reported the new sum to the bookkeeper, who accepted it. Several days later a committee meeting was called to determine the distribution of monthly loans. One of the Department officials was at the meeting, and in order to allocate the loans properly, he suggested that they be based upon the amount of produce previously shipped; thus he asked that each person's account be read out. When they reached Masoud's account, the overly large amount of onions was discovered, and with it, a complex chain of events proceeded to unfold.

Masoud had planted onions with his brother-in-law, who was his neighbor. But his brother-in-law's account listed two tons, not four; since they were partners, how could one man report twice what the other did? The brother-in-law was standing outside, listening through the window; he burst into the room immediately and asked how such a difference could exist. Neither Masoud nor the instructor felt that they could answer, particularly with the Department official present. They mumbled some vague explanations, but the cat was out of the bag: it was apparent that the accounts had been improperly altered.

The next day the story was all over the village; Masoud and his brother-in-law were on bad terms, so the latter enjoyed telling the story. Once again Masoud was accused of cheating. But this time the accusation was more serious: the rumor spread that Masoud had been altering the accounts and that he had been splitting his profits with the committee members and the instructors. This was a very serious charge, and tension quickly mounted.

The story broke on Wednesday night. Saturday morning, at the synagogue, there was a near riot. The Levis sensed immediately that this issue was exploitable; they pressed the attack against Masoud and the committee. The committee members —the Dehans and their supporters—answered with shouts and counteraccusations. Several fist fights broke out. Many people were convinced of the theft. Masoud had obviously been stealing; that was the secret of his farming success! Everyone began to recall incidents when they were certain they had sent large quantities to market and later discovered a much smaller sum credited in their account. They suspected that Masoud had been rearranging the accounts to his own advantage for many months. Sentiment against the committee was growing.

The Levis insisted that a general meeting be held that evening. Everyone agreed, and it was decided to convene before the weekly movie. Later in the afternoon, the Levis came to the instructor's house and invited him to attend the meeting. They began to discuss the entire incident. But the discussion quickly turned into a raging argument. The instructor was angry at the allegation that he had been stealing from the village; the Levis did not say that the instructors had stolen, but they continued to intimate it.

The meeting began immediately after the evening prayers. All the male members were present, dressed in their Sabbath best. The Levis and their followers again accused the committee members of complicity in the "onion scandal" and demanded that a new committee be elected. The instructor, who until then had been silent, jumped to his feet and asked if anyone was accusing him of theft. One of the Levis answered affirmatively, and the two began shouting at each other. The instructor finally marched out of the room and challenged Levi to come with him. Levi accepted the challenge, but others held him back. The instructor, however, had left the meeting.

The Levis continued to demand a new election. Many of the unaffiliated spoke for it. The Calahs also supported them. Seeing that the tide was turning against them, and perhaps also foreseeing the final outcome, the committee members agreed to a new election. Nominations for the new committee began. Immediately, the Levis and Paros began to nominate one another: they now saw a chance to regain control of the village. The other settlers, however, perceived their intentions. While many were angry over the account switching, they had no illusions regarding the Levis' rule; they recalled the long battle to unseat them from power. Thus, one after the other, people began filing out of the room; the movie had meanwhile begun. In a short time, everyone had left except the Levis and Paros. Their attempt to capture control was, for the moment, unsuccessful.

No one in the village imagined that the struggle was really over, however. The Levis had failed; but, given the nature of life at Oren, one could safely predict that there would soon be more crises and new chances to grasp power.

What are the implications of these incidents for community life? How do politics influence village social alignments?

The community was jarred regularly by such crises. A general sense of discouragement and a lowering of morale often followed the incidents. How could one imagine his future in a village in which conflict constantly erupts, and where accusation and distrust were commonplace? The villagers viewed the future with uncertainty and sensed that their community was unstable.

Tensions were multiplied by these incidents. Irritation and anger built up and were then focused upon different persons or groups. Masoud, for example, became the target for widespread attacks, as others had before him. The political system had, in effect, a dual function in regard to community tension. Political antagonisms—such as the struggle between the Levi and Dehan factions—generated tensions between community members. The entire village was drawn into these contests, as envy and personal distrust mounted in intensity. Politics, therefore, were tension provoking. At the same time, however, the political system provided outlets for expressing aggression in a controlled manner. The village meetings were regular occasions for venting anger and irritation; they were inevitably long, confused shouting matches. Although at times they veered toward violence, these public meetings had the effect of providing public forums for channeling aggression.

Most important, these events emphasized how politics divided the social structure of the village but, at the same time, reinforced the different social units. Intergroup conflict made the community splintered and weak, but the units within it became strengthened. The Levis and their followers, the Dehan families and their supporters, Masoud and his family, Yaacov Calah and his kin, all of these groups acted as unified, cooperating units. Since the kin groups were the primary political units, they in particular became strengthened. Moments of calm might separate them; specific issues might divide them; but in a political struggle, the kin groups rejoined and stood together.

The community as a whole was also sometimes united. Conflict frequently took the form of *moshav*–Settlement Department or settler–instructor struggles. During these contests, internal dissensions were forgotten, and the village assumed a united front. Such moments were brief, however; new crises arose, and old quarrels erupted anew. The internal allegiances tended to reassert themselves. While there was an enveloping and shrinking of alignments, the kin groups, the dominant social forms, remained the primary social and political groups.

There is still another conclusion—more properly, a hypothesis —that is suggested by this analysis. Political organization at Oren featured a "two-party" system: either the Dehan or the Levi factions dominated the village committee, and a change in control meant replacing one of these groups by the other. No other permanent faction emerged. Although there were sometimes loose confederations of families, these alliances were normally short-lived and did not threaten the control of the two kinship-based groups. This "two party" system was based upon the village's social composition: the numerical superiority of the two large kinship groups. Their constituents—that is, kinsmen plus their allies—gave each group a substantial, dependable base of support. Moreover, this particular crystallization was reinforced by the position of the village leaders: the two most authoritative villagers were also the heads of the two kinship units. There were no other settlers whose talents were attractive enough to mobilize another faction. (Sephardi had earlier organized a faction around his leadership, it will be recalled, but his position crumbled before the opposition of one of the kinship groups and the village instructors.) This distribution of authority may therefore be seen as reinforcing the polarization of the village into two competing "parties."

This particular pattern—the coupling of large factions with persuasive leaders—could have a stabilizing effect upon the village: alternatives were limited, and any combining and recombining of groups was therefore held in check. Conflicts existed between the two factions, but this particular polarity also offered the possibility of sustained control by one faction or another. In other words, from this viewpoint Oren's political organization had positive implications for community-wide stability.

This hypothesis suggests a number of additional problems. How is village control maintained in communities that lack a "two-party" system? What happens when factions are more numerous or when powerful leaders lack a dependable base of support?

These latter issues can, once again, be profitably studied by comparing Oren with the neighboring village, Shikma. At Shikma, it will be recalled, half of the villagers did not belong to kinship units, and the kinship groups tend to be small in size. In addition, the two dominant community figures, Machlouf and Daniel, were not linked to other settlers by bonds of kinship.

In contrast with Oren, the factions at Shikma were smaller, more numerous, and based upon different principles. Four more or less clearly separate factions were present in the village. The two largest included fourteen and seven members each. As at Oren, each of the groups was centered around a set of kinsmen; not all faction members were kinsmen, but the group's permanent core was composed of persons bound by family ties. Both groups were led by young or middle-aged males. The authority of these leaders was, however, generally limited to the faction itself; while influential within their own faction, among other villagers, their following was more restricted. As was noted previously, kinship ties were associated with rural origins, and these groups at Shikma were predominantly rural.

The two other factions were quite different. They were based, in essence, upon powerful leadership rather than family or kin ties: what joined people to one another was allegiance to a strong personality. Daniel and Machlouf were the leaders of these groups. Their factions were numerically small; one numbered four families, and the other, seven. Yet, although their permanent following was small, both Machlouf and Daniel were authoritative figures throughout the village. Their administrative ability, energy, and persuasive talents often enabled them to join persons and groups together into larger blocs. Both men had served as village secretary, and both were experienced in representing the community to outside agencies. Their personal relations were typically stormy: each bitterly fought the other for control of the village. In contrast with the other two factions, their support came from among the "urbanized" settlers.

The four factions were fairly stable units. Their memberships were relatively constant, though there was some shifting of support from one group to another. These factions did not, however, represent Shikma's entire population: the four factions comprised thirty-two settlers, while another sixteen were not included among them. These sixteen villagers, almost all of whom were "isolated urban families," formed a loose, floating body that did not pledge regular support to any faction. For several years they had backed Daniel, but later, this support was mainly withdrawn and partially transferred to Machlouf. In many cases, the support of these unaffiliated settlers was decisive: they created a majority by joining one or another faction.

This combination of numerous factions, aggressive leaders heading small groups, and a large body of unattached persons produced a fluid and highly volatile situation. No single faction was large enough to dominate the community and its councils. Indeed, no two factions together constituted a majority. The kinship-based factional groups were comparatively large. However, neither boasted a leader who was accepted throughout the village or who was able to attract others and organize them into a stable bloc. Lacking community-wide leadership, these two groups were unable to dominate the village. On the other hand, the two more powerful personalities, Daniel and Machlouf, were not supported by any large, permanent corps of supporters. The four groups therefore stood in opposition to one another, as each struggled to gain influence and representation in community affairs. Factions joined one another, Machlouf and Daniel organized individuals and groups into their "parties," and all of the factional heads sought to attract the third of the village which had no permanent allegiance. Various constellations were then formed: Daniel's group joined forces with the larger kinship unit or Machlouf rallied many of the unaffiliated together with a smaller kinship group. These confederations were normally short-lived, however, and tended to break and form again periodically.

The typical situation at Shikma was therefore one of fractionalism, turbulence, and unrest. The village was splintered, and no political combination was able to weld the community together. At Shikma consensus appeared to be unattainable, and internal divisions did not permit community-wide cohesion or a feeling of village unity.

Comparing political organization at Oren and Shikma indicates that village political and social stability depends upon such factors as the number and size of competing political units, as well as the distribution of authority within the community. Even though Oren was often torn by factional disputes, the village "two-party" system may have been advantageous for the establishment of long-term village stability. On the other hand, the division of authority at Shikma contributed to recurrent political instability and social unrest. Differences in social solidarity—that is, differences in group formation and the alignment of groups with village leaders—may thus be seen to be of crucial importance for village social, political, and economic development. These issues, seen in furthur comparative perspective, will again be considered in the concluding chapter.

CHAPTER VI

Oren as an Administered Community

OREN was earlier described as an "administered community":
the village's social, cultural, economic, and political development
was directly determined by outside agencies. Planning groups,
rather than the villagers themselves, initiated and directed important phases of community life. Policies framed by outside groups
determined, for example, who would live in the village, what its
organization would be, or the rate of capital investment. How
these plans were implemented, and the degree to which they
were successfully carried out, influenced the village's growth.

Some facets of this situation were presented in previous chapters. In discussing the establishment of the village, attention centered upon how the settlement authorities formed the original
village group and how the immigrants were initiated into
moshav life. Two chapters described the planning apparatus itself and indicated ways in which the administrative system influenced the village's social and political life. Two additional features of administered village life are presented in this chapter,
namely, the impact paternalistic practices had upon the villagers

and their reactions to paternalism; and the reformist features of the settlement program, and, in particular, the cultural activities of the village instructors.

Paternalism is a dominant characteristic of the administrator-settler relationship. As was earlier pointed out, village programs were normally drawn up without actively consulting the villagers. When new crops were introduced, village buildings constructed, or new credit systems instituted, the decisions were made at district or national levels and then announced to the settlers. Since the Settlement Department held title to most of the village capital and was the villagers' chief creditor, it was free to propose new programs. Moreover, inasmuch as the villagers were new immigrants, unfamiliar with farming and *moshav* life, the Department claimed better understanding of the settlers' real interests: Department personnel, veteran, experienced Israelis, believed that they understood the settlers' needs better than the settlers themselves. The aim of the settlement program was village independence, but the Department believed that this could best be achieved by intensive guidance, followed by a gradual relinquishing of real power to the settlers.

Paternalism had various results. Feeling themselves powerless to control the system, some settlers accepted it; at the same time, others resisted and struggled against the system or sought to influence it by subversion. Both reactions were common, and each needs to be explored in detail.

Dependence as a principle of social organization and an outlook upon life has important antecedents in the organization of Jewish life in Morocco. Moroccan society in general was hierarchically organized: both as a community and as individuals, the Jews' fortunes depended upon the acts of the ruling Muslims. Within the *millah* itself power was reserved for the rabbis and the rich; social mobility often depended upon the good will of these persons. Moreover, the French colonizers and administrators assumed positions of control throughout most of Morocco;

Jews were sometimes their assistants, but usually they assumed subservient positions. The *moshav* and settlement system tended to reinforce these feelings: not only was Oren a dependent community, each settler was often in the position of a suppliant. A settler's success was very much bound up with the acts of those in power.

During the first years, few settlers imagined that they might succeed by themselves: the *moshav* and the settlement system were too new, complex, and difficult to understand and control. The villagers recognized their lack of experience in farming; without persistent instruction and guidance their farming efforts would most likely fail. They did not know the language adequately, nor did they have managerial training; without these essential skills, how could they themselves direct complex community affairs? From their first day in Israel various groups cared for them; the Department officials had organized the community, and they continually made additional capital investments. The fact that instructors were attached to the village also strengthened these dependent feelings. Village instructors held the dominant positions, and their behavior often gave the settlers a sense of impotence; they implied and often acted as if they held the keys to success. Dependence also had many rewards: by accepting their situation the settlers received costly equipment and many skilled services. For all of these reasons, many were reluctant to act independently and often preferred to follow the officials' directions. When the Department executives asked the villagers to help in the negotiations regarding Oren's onion crop, it will be recalled that the settlers refused. Where would they go, what would they say, and who would listen to them? Moreover, they said, it was the Department's responsibility and not theirs.

The settler who accepted the system did not seek to shape his own fate; instead, he turned to others. This attitude is well expressed in the immigrants' ideal of the "protector." Many were

strongly convinced that in order to succeed they must find a
protector—"someone who will care for us." Without such a
guardian, they imagined that their personal efforts would fail;
what counted was not so much personal striving but rather the
continuous assistance of the powerful. The protector image was
best fulfilled by a veteran Israeli—one who had influence in the
controlling bureaucracies and who also identified with the immigrants' plight. Such a person might be called upon in moments
of crisis, and it was expected that he would solve the settlers'
problems. In many instances the Settlement Department officials
filled, or were expected to fill, this role: the village instructor, or
the District head, was thus cast in the image of the traditional
Moroccan *cheikh*.

The settlers were at times able to find satisfying protector relations: they became convinced that some of the instructors and
executives had their personal interests in mind. These persons
were warmly regarded and became the object of discussion and
adulation. There were, however, serious strains inherent in such
a relationship. Not all of the Department workers encouraged
the protector image; some did not attempt to enter into personal
relationships, and the reputations of others were damaged by inefficiency (either real or imagined). Moreover, since personal
ties were crucial to such a relation, it was difficult to make the
situation general. Close ties were often achieved with the village
instructor; since they lived in the village, the instructors were
well known. But instructors changed frequently; a settler just
began to get acquainted with an instructor when he left and
someone else replaced him. Moreover, from the instructor's
point of view, friendships could be dangerous, since they implied
favoritism.

The village instructor was only one link in the settlement
chain; while his tasks were important, his range of influence was
limited. Key policy issues were decided far from the village—in
Jerusalem, Tel Aviv, or Beersheba. On this higher level, the set-

tlers not only lacked information, but they had no direct, personal contact. Higher echelon executives and planners sometimes visited the village; this happened especially during village crises, when key officials arrived for brief consultations. But these persons and their intentions were remote from the villagers; their personalities were unknown, and lasting ties were never formed with them. Thus the settlers did not always succeed in finding a protector, nor were they certain that the officials really cared. If the settlers sought personal ties, how could they find them in a bureaucracy, where personnel changed and an institution, not a personality, was stressed? How could one depend upon persons unknown or feel real security in the sudden, crisis-provoked visits?

The villagers' relations with Department personnel were also affected by cultural differences between the two groups: settlement officials were all (or nearly all) of European origin, while the settlers were, of course, non-Europeans. This feature of the settlement structure had various implications. The settlers conceived the executives as representing an elite group—a group that had different advantages and expectations, as well as different behavior norms. The manner of speech, the attitudes, and the behavior of this group differentiated it from village society. Moreover, the settlers also recognized the general ethnic stratification which characterizes Israeli society: high status positions are monopolized by *Ashkenazim* (persons of European origin), while *Sepharadim* (those of Middle Eastern descent) hold lower prestige posts.[1] This fact, among others, led the villagers to sense discrimination against them; they were convinced that, in situations of choice, Europeans always received preference. "For us Moroccans, there is only the *moshav;* when we came they told us that we must become farmers. But what happens when a Jew

[1] This subject is discussed in A. Weingrod, "The Two Israels," *Commentary,* XXX, No. 4 (1962), and in his *Israel: A Study in Group Relations* (New York: Praeger, 1965).

comes from Rumania? He goes to Tel Aviv and is given a good job!" As this comment indicates, the settlers were strongly convinced that favors usually went to others and that they were discriminated against because they were Moroccan.

This sense of cultural difference was often a barrier to the development of intimate relations between villagers and the settlement personnel. Although it did not hinder dependence upon them—the settlers believed that Europeans were more likely to succeed and that a Moroccan, "like ourselves," would fail—the feeling did limit personal relations and thereby inhibited the protector relationship. In some cases, of course, prolonged contact did result in close ties. In these cases the settlers said jokingly, "He's a Moroccan," as an expression of their trust and admiration. But these relationships were exceptional.

Acceptance and dependence were one phase of the settlers' reaction to paternalism; resistance and subversion were another. The settlers resisted plans and proposals when they did not meet their own interests, when they did not understand the plans, or when they grew tired and disillusioned by the entire system. The Department personnel proposed policies and then sought to convert the settlers to their point of view. For their part, the settlers might refuse to accept the plans or hold out for better terms. The results of this process were a long series of conflicts between the Department and the settlers.

The villagers quickly developed various tactics in their negotiations with the Department. Rejecting plans was itself a powerful tactic, and the settlers often employed it. The villagers learned that, in their kind of settlement, cooperation was essential, and that if they withdrew it, the entire endeavor would suffer. After all, they alone tended the crops and lived in the village; many others might be engaged in service operations, but carrying out the programs depended upon their labor. They also knew that it was unlikely for Department support to be permanently withdrawn; for in this system, the Department was the partner most deeply concerned. The planners and administrators not only had a natural interest in the realization of their projects, they were also ideologically committed to the ideals of land settlement, immigrant absorption, and population dispersion. Thus, they were bound to the programs by national ideals as well as more personal interests—for them the villages had a national significance. Simply by being uncooperative—by rejecting suggested quotas or prices—the settlers exercised a strong force: they were able to turn the paternalistic nature of the venture to their own advantage. Certain that they would not be abandoned, the settlers rejected Department plans and later sought to bargain and negotiate. Such negotiations involved many meetings and various personnel: the village was represented by the committee members and other influential persons, and the Department negotiators included regional and District executives. These meetings were always lengthy, and often they grew increasingly bitter. Generally speaking, the differences ended in compromise: both sides agreed to accept some middle course.

Threats of heavy penalties were often leveled against the settlers, but they were usually not carried out. Like the settlers who were ambivalent, veering between acceptance and resistance, the Department moved between a "hard" and "soft" line. These shifts in policy resulted in confusion and unrest: the settlers were uncertain of how the Department officials would react, and they could never tell when threats would be enforced or if they were simply part of the bargaining process. When, after many threats, the Department did impose penalties, the settlers were invariably shocked and annoyed. Why did the authorities act sternly in this instance? Uncertainty added a note of tension to an already charged relationship.

There were additional ways in which the settlers resisted Department plans. For example, they sometimes brought their grievances into the public arena in an effort to mobilize general support. This course of action was sometimes successful; news-

paper stories that reported the plight and sorry conditions of the
new immigrants—and of autocratic officials who failed to serve
them properly—generated sympathy for the settlers and brought
pressure to bear upon the Department. To cite one instance of
this technique, during the long struggle for power between the
Dehan and Levi families, the Levis managed to have an interview
printed in one of the daily papers in which they attacked the
village committee and the Department for improper management
of Oren's affairs. The Department was particularly sensitive to
public criticism, and news accounts could influence its policies.

The settlers also sought to turn the various bureaucracies, or
different levels of the same organization, against each other. For
example, if their demands were refused on a regional level, they
might apply to District officers; if their efforts were not successful among the District personnel, they turned to national executives. Since there was sometimes lack of coordination between
these groups—and since the pressures placed on different levels
had different results—this tactic might succeed. (A settler
demonstration staged in the Department's regional Beersheba
headquarters usually had little effect; the offices were on a side
street, and since the demonstrations were frequent, they attracted little attention. However, if the settlers demonstrated in
front of the Department's Jerusalem headquarters, they were
likely to receive publicity, and their demands would at least partially be met.) The settlers might also turn to the settlement
movement for aid. While this sometimes proved effective, the
results were usually negligible, since the movement and the Department cooperated with one another. As a last resort, the settlers also appealed to other political parties: that is, the villagers
threatened and in fact turned to other political parties for support. Since the religious political parties had a permanent "representative" within Oren—the synagogue and sometimes the
schools were controlled by the Ministry of Religion and thus by
the religious parties—this threat was convincing. Once entered

into, however, party intrigues tended to become uncontrolled, and because the issues were fought between the parties, the results were often to the settlers' own ultimate detriment. (Oren, in common with other *moshavim,* could not change its political affiliation: if the settlers wished to affiliate formally with a different party, they had to leave the village. The village was the "property" of the settlement movement and consequently of a political party, and its political ties could not be changed. There was an informal agreement between the parties, and "raiding," except during election time, rarely took place.)

Attitudes of acceptance and resistance alternately dominated in the village. Many settlers, however, found a simpler solution to the complexities of village-Department relations: they silently subverted plans and sought, on a small or larger scale, to "milk the system." These villagers sought out the uncontrolled areas in the administered system and turned them to their own personal advantage. The private garden plots and the private sale of produce are classic instances of this technique: the settlers accepted the Department capital and then used it in ways that they themselves chose. There are many examples of this technique. When, for example, the Department wished to introduce chicken farming into the village, more than half of the settlers registered to receive chicken coops and chickens. After the coops had been built, however, most at first refused to accept the chickens. What these settlers wanted was an additional structure to store hay and seed, not the new problems of chicken raising. To cite another method, some settlers were able to channel money allocated to the villages to their own private use. The settler charged with organizing nightly guard duty registered himself as a watchman every night, whether or not he actually stood guard. These instances of subversion placed additional strains upon the *moshav*-Department relationship: the Department framed more rigid programs and acted to obstruct settler subversion.

At different times, and in varied circumstances, these poses—
acceptance, resistance, and subversion—were chosen by the villagers. All of the settlers resisted some Department programs,
some tended to take a more acceptant attitude, and practically
all practiced some form of subversion. While the attitude
shifted, certain of the practices became associated with particular groups. The Levi families were leaders in most resistance
programs: they led the village in rejecting Department policies
and demanded a larger measure of independence. Members of
this group possessed managerial skills as well as initiative and energy, and they desired to take an independent course. Moreover,
they did not spurn drastic techniques: the Levis publicized their
grievances in the press, and they openly turned to other political
parties. On the other hand, the Dehans usually assumed a more
acceptant, cooperative attitude: they were pliable, willing to go
along with the Department's suggestions. The Dehan leaders
were of the opinion that cooperation was a desired tactic in the
Department-settler relation: the settlers would benefit more by
accepting Department plans, whereas resistance would lead to
conflict and little advantage. In this attitude they were joined by
most of the middle-aged and older settlers. These men who were
not active in public affairs and did not fully grasp the *moshav*
situation tended toward acceptance. The contrasts in attitudes
between the Levis and Dehans in part reflected personality
differences between the leaders of both groups: Moshe Dehan
was a somewhat permissive, yielding person, while Shimon Levi
was more aggressive and tended to be autocratic.

Within the village, the political fortunes of these two groups
was also affected by their position regarding Department policy:
the other villagers supported the Dehans so long as cooperation
yielded results, but they were attracted to the Levis' activism
when acceptance appeared against their interests. The villagers
themselves had different opinions as to which tactics were more
effective: some argued that quiet acceptance was more fruitful,

while others were convinced that resistance alone brought better results. The successful execution of Department policies therefore influenced the village's political alignments: for example, if policies proposed by the Department and accepted by the Dehans failed, then the latter group might be removed from office and replaced by others. Community leadership depended upon the leading group's ability to deliver the promised programs; since the community was administered, this primarily meant the degree to which the Department fulfilled its commitments. The village sociopolitical system was therefore influenced by this coupling of village groups with Department policies.

The Department's paternalism profoundly affected Oren's development. Faced with a situation of training new immigrants in farming and village life, the Department imposed a directed type of community. Such a system was bound to encourage feelings of dependence among the settlers—the Department appeared all-powerful, and many were anxious to accept its direction. The authorities themselves wished to maintain dominance. The protector image was, in fact, a realistic appraisal of the settlement system; since the village depended so heavily upon the activities of the settlement bureaucracies, personal ties were likely to have direct benefits, or, at least, they lent an allusion of interest and potential assistance.

The system also placed effective powers in the hands of the settlers themselves. The Department held the preponderance of power, yet it rarely used extreme penalties. For example, credit might be withheld from settlers who marketed their produce individually, but negotiation always resulted in further extensions. The settlers were therefore able to manipulate the system and to turn it to their own advantage. In this sense, the settlement system was flexible, and settler pressure might influence Department policy. Moreover, this manipulation introduced the immigrants to the conventions of Israeli politics; while dependent, they also learned how to operate within the Israeli institutional structure. The type of paternalism practiced in the village—all-embracing guidance and direction, yet open to resistance and compromise—led the settlers to understand and also to take advantage of the system. In this sense, the administered system was an important learning experience.[2]

Relations between the settlers and the Department personnel were never smooth. As has been emphasized throughout this description, there were recurrent failures in the system: planning errors, such as the "onion incident," led to disturbances in village life. As has also been indicated, these crises were nearly shattering. However, at the same time they emphasized the links between the settlers and the administrators. While the settlers felt remote and dependent, they also recognized, however dimly, their participation within a larger structure of ideas and persons. Instructors and other personnel changed, yet the settlers knew them, or of them, and they were often persuaded that the officials did "care" and that they had the settlers' interests in mind. Moreover, a sense of joint task was sometimes successfully transmitted: the many quarrels, the long drawn out negotiations between the settlement authorities and the settlers, were themselves partially carried on within an aura of joint participation. They were developed, at least in the beginning stages, within an atmosphere of familiarity and even joviality. While the conflicts often later developed more extreme overtones, each party first recognized the other's position and then jockeyed for control within the limits of the situation.

Conflict itself, whether mild or impassioned, provided regular channels of communication and contact. Conflict implies social relationships, a known status system, and the exchange of information and sentiments. In the cases outlined earlier, disagree-

[2] This same conclusion is reached by Dorothy Willner, and is discussed in her article, "Politics and Change in Israel: The Case of Land Settlement," *Human Organization,* **XXIV,** No. 1 (1965).

ments between the settlers and the officials resulted in a series of formal meetings. Officials on the various levels and different settlers participated. Each crisis provoked similar meetings. The relations between the parties were often stormy, but the meetings themselves were repetitive. The contestants struggled, yet they regularly met one another. Moreover, the meetings tended to be intense encounters, as anger and frustration poured forth. This very intensity personalized and deepened the relationships. Conflicts thus provided the basis for relationships, however tenuous: the villagers became participants within a larger social system.

This analysis of village direction has thus far focused upon the system of planning and some of its consequences. In addition to these efforts, the village authorities were engaged in a broad program of directed culture change. This program of reform was a distinctive feature of the settlement system. Indeed, the settlement project was itself an expression of the general Israeli desire for rapid culture change. Cultural innovations were proposed, and what is more, concerted efforts were made to resocialize the immigrants. How this program was implemented is considered in the remaining portion of this chapter.

From the point of view of the settlement authorities, the new immigrants at Oren were considered to be "primitive persons" (the word "primitive" has become part of the Israeli lexicon). This label was exceedingly influential: it rationalized and guided broad areas of institutional and personal behavior. Generally speaking, all immigrants from non-Western countries were labeled "primitive": whether they came from Yemen, Morocco, Kurdistan, Tunisia, or India, they were all *primitivim*. From the perspective of the European directing groups, there might be levels of primitivism: settlers from Kurdistan, for example, were popularly considered to be more "primitive" than Moroccans. On the other hand, Moroccans themselves were categorized into groups: the more "advanced" were labeled "Casablanca," whereas the less Westernized were known as "Atlas Mountaineers." These were, however, only gradations within a type: all the immigrants were more or less primitive.

This image illustrates the underlying philosophy of reform. The label "primitive" is obviously not ennobling; it is a damaging social category. One who is "primitive" is behind or beneath someone who is "advanced." The concept of reform, it will be recalled, was one of the basic assumptions of the veteran culture: given the proper tools, the correct approach, and appropriate pressures, personalities might be reformed. This faith underlay the settlement project. Since the settlers were "primitive," and since this condition was undesirable, the settlers must be changed. "We want to make them into Israelis" was the often voiced, classic definition of this aspect of the settlement program.

Along with the program of village economic and political direction, a program of cultural reform emerged. It envisioned two allied goals: first, the settlers were to become Western-type persons, and second, they were to assume the ideals and modes of behavior enunciated in the *moshav*. The village instructors, the schools, and other national institutions, all became agents in this program for change.

The village instructors had a primary role in the movement for reform. By virtue of their living in the village, they were ever-present symbols of Israeli culture. Their dress, manners, and daily behavior represented the new life to be learned and led. The instructors were models, and they were often copied. For example, instructors generally dressed informally, in shorts and khaki shirts, and were normally bareheaded, except when working in the sun; many settlers learned to wear similar dress, and only the very old among them retained the traditional Moroccan *jellaba*. The settlers continued to wear hats as a symbol of their religiosity, but these were usually Israeli-style hats of a type commonly worn. If there were both male and female instructors in the village, their relations were usually informal; for example, they might live in the same house, sleeping in different rooms. This informality between the sexes was also influential, particularly for the younger, unmarried settlers, who sought to model male-female relations upon the instructor's example. If the instructor was married, his household became an important reference point: the villagers copied his furnishings, adopted similar household items (a refrigerator or gas range), and imitated the observed relationships between husband and wife. If he had children, the instructor's child-rearing practices also became a model for parent-child relations.

In addition to this imitative process, some instructors consciously set out to direct the immigrants to new forms of behavior. This spirit was strongest during the initial settlement period, immediately after the first families reached Oren. Not only were the immigrants themselves confused by the new situation and thus easily influenced, the first group of instructors conceived their task as actively initiating broad cultural changes. These youngsters were part of a movement that recruited instructors from the older, veteran *moshavim;* for them an instructor's work centered mainly around introducing new, Israeli traditions. Although the groups of instructors that later served at Oren shared these attitudes, they tended to intervene less in the settlers' family affairs and generally adopted a more professional role. Yet, cases of personal intervention characterized the instructors' work throughout Oren's history. Numerous examples may be cited. Seeing an old woman working in the fields, the instructor insisted that she be sent home: old women should not labor in the sun. Hearing that a settler had beaten his wife, the instructor castigated the husband: in Israel women are not beaten. If he entered a house in which flies swarmed about the garbage-covered floor, the instructor insisted that the settler clean and repair his home: dirt leads to illness. In other situations the *madrich* might urge that an "Israeli name" be given a new-born child: Eitan or Ofrah were better suited to the new situation than Masoud or Rachel.

The instructors sought also to introduce a different cultural outlook. The instructor represented the essentially secular traditions of farming Israel; the immigrants, of course, were traditionally religious persons, and the instructors tried in various ways to convey their own secular attitudes. For example, it will be recalled that the instructors never attended the synagogue services; their absence from prayers was conscious and pointed. An instructor might also debate the question of religious behavior with the settlers. The issue of orthodoxy versus secularism was of great concern to the men at Oren. Many of the settlers were uncertain regarding the proper range of their religious practice. The instructors' example was powerful and attractive; it seemed to typify the path to the new life.

In their efforts to introduce change, the instructors normally had a select audience: their influence was greatest among the unmarried men and the young married settlers. There are various reasons for this selective appeal. The instructors were themselves young, and there was a mutual attraction between persons who had at least age in common. The young settlers and the instructors maintained visiting relations—the villagers congregated at the instructor's home—and they sometimes organized joint excursions. Since the younger villagers were more conversant in Hebrew, they were more open to outside influence. Moreover, the young men were less tied to tradition and more receptive to new ideas: these shifts had already been evident in Morocco, and they became intensified in Israel. On the other hand, the older settlers mastered Hebrew slowly, if at all, and tended to be conservative; there were few informal contacts between the instructors and settlers over the age of thirty-five. This latter group was primarily concerned with earning a living, and with home and family; they had little in common with the instructors, and their relations were largely of an instrumental kind. Besides, according to the settlement ideology, the aged were the "desert generation," from whom only negligible results could be anticipated. It was thus the young who were most influenced by the instructors. Among them their impact was greatest.

The village school was another agent of change. Children from the ages of six to fourteen went to the school organized in a neighboring village. Children were required by law to attend elementary school; since education was free, most of them regularly attended classes. As is typical of immigration situations, the school sought to introduce many changes. Most of the children entered knowing little if any Hebrew; in the daily classes they began to master the language, learning to write and read as well as to speak properly. The curriculum also included studies about Israel—its history, current problems, and daily events. The children were thus made aware of the new world about them. The teachers conveyed subtler kinds of learning as well: they encouraged the children to be clean and neat, to speak the truth and never to use force, to respect and cooperate with their classmates. The teachers were usually young—between the ages of twenty and thirty—and most of them were of European origin; they became, or sought to become, models for the children.

Most teachers were not content simply to teach new skills: they preferred to teach new ideas and attitudes, the new way of life. "If only we could take the children away from here, away from their homes and families, and place them in an Israeli atmosphere, then they would truly change!" So thought the teachers, for, from their point of view, the home influence restricted the school's effectiveness. The teachers were somewhat pessimistic regarding the outcome of their work: the few school years, during which time the children remained under the influence of the home, were not sufficient to resocialize the youngsters.

There was, in fact, a striking difference between those youngsters who lived at home and attended the village school, and the few children who lived at or attended larger educational institutions away from the village. The three youngsters who were members of *aliyat noar* groups and who received training in a *kibbutz* exhibited many signs of acculturation. Away from home except for holidays and week-end visits, they were under the continuous influence of new kinds of ideas and values. These young people learned Hebrew well; they spoke fluently, without much trace of a Moroccan accent. They knew the general Israeli world and learned to move freely within it; in large measure they identified with the new culture, though they still might feel restricted within it. Their dress, bearing, and in large measure behavior and attitude, was not a duplication of their parents'; in part, at least, they had become "Israelis."

Resocialization was also associated with army service and training. Although only six of the young men completed their army training, this experience had important educational effects. Army service extends over a two-and-a-half-year period, generally beginning at about the age of eighteen. Women as well as men are required to serve, though girls may opt out of service if they claim religious affiliation or are married. Thus far, none of the girls at Oren served in the army and only a few of the eligible boys entered the service. Those who did serve, however, learned new skills and different modes of behavior. During army service they mastered Hebrew, and their training took them to different parts of the country. They also received training in special skills—cooking, driving, electrical maintenance, and so forth. Furthermore, the army itself made a pointed effort to inculcate the immigrant youth with new cultural attitudes. Group behavior was modeled after the veteran officers, themselves native Israelis or Europeans. Since the recruits were largely removed from other influences, this intense experience often resulted in personality reformation. When the young men returned home to the village, they appeared as different persons: they had, in part at least, become resocialized.

In addition to this general "Westernization" movement, there was another front upon which the program for change operated: the attempt to indoctrinate the settlers with the *moshav* ideals and practices. The concepts taught were essentially those of the "classic *moshav*"—the cooperative as first developed by East European immigrants. Thus, for example, the immigrants were expected to learn to work and to grant equality to their fellow villagers; to cooperate within the community and assist one another in time of need; and it was expected that they would practice a system of democratic government and concern themselves with the needs of the community as a whole.

The settlers daily experienced the *moshav* system; as has already been suggested, they accepted parts of it, rejected other parts, and transformed still other aspects. In addition to this direct experience, the village instructors attempted to inculcate *moshav* principles upon the immigrants. For example, some agricultural instructors worked in the fields. Laboring side by side with the new immigrants, they sought to demonstrate by personal example the "goodness of labor." Many instructors spent long hours explaining new techniques.

Moshav equality was taught in several ways. All of the homes in the village were originally of equal size, and so were the plots of land allotted to each settler. Moreover, when capital goods were allocated, the instructors usually advised that equal division be made: each settler should have an equal opportunity. Independent achievement, another *moshav* principle, was furthered by the instructors' distribution of monthly loans. It will be recalled that these loans were usually scaled according to each settler's diligence and success in tending his crops. In minor matters the instructor urged the settlers to solve their own problems. A settler who had not received some commodity, or who felt that mistakes had been made in his accounts, was urged to check and solve the problem himself.

Much time and effort was expended in the attempt to teach the *moshav* cooperative principles: the settlement authorities conceived of the cooperative arrangements as the essential aspect of the new way of life. Since formal cooperation was expressed in community-wide purchasing and marketing, the *madrichim* wanted to convince the settlers of the usefulness of these arrangements. A settler who marketed his produce privately was verbally chastised; more stringent methods, such as withholding loans, were also used. The instructors made use of various public and private opportunities to lecture the settlers regarding the value of community cooperation: it was only by joining together, they urged, that the individual settler received maximum benefits.

During the weekly committee meetings and the more irregular village gatherings, the instructors attempted to teach the forms and traditions of democratic government. A settler was usually chairman of the meeting, and the instructors often deliberately attempted to involve the villagers in the debate. Teaching democracy was, however, a complex task: democratic forms were followed, but, as was earlier made clear, real responsibility was not generally granted to the settlers. The instructors desired participation and real community direction, yet they feared error. Many meetings were called, and heated discussions took place; but the more important decisions were made by the settlement authorities, not the villagers.

The program for cultural change may thus be seen to have proceeded on different levels: there were pressures within the village, guided by the instructors and the school; and there were systems and situations outside the community where individual young persons had left home and became "resocialized." These pressures were powerful and continuous. Two general conclusions may be drawn regarding these efforts. First, it is important to stress that the program for change was aimed almost exclusively at the younger generation of settlers and their children. Insofar as such programs were deliberately developed, or informal contacts applied, they pertained primarily to the younger settlers. This selective approach increased the potential for conflict between the generations. Immigration itself, as well as the demands of *moshav* life, had placed strains upon traditional social relationships. The old system of authority was challenged and began to shift. The resocialization program added to these pressures. It was a major factor leading to the reorganization of family and group relations.

Second, it should be noted that the immigrants exhibited a generally positive attitude toward the change program. There was a widespread feeling among the settlers that new adaptations were required. The settlers recognized and expressed the idea that Israeli conditions were different from their previous experience and that they needed to make some accommodations to these conditions. As immigrants in a new land, they perceived an inadequacy in their own traditions and were prepared to attempt new forms of behavior. Thus, for example, the village instructors' intervention in matters of personal behavior was not only often accepted, it was also sometimes sought after: the instructors were appealed to as mediators in highly intimate disputes. There was, of course, some diversity in adaptation: not all of the settlers were equally amenable to change, and only some types of innovations were accepted. These differential reactions to change form the topic of the next chapter. It is important to stress, however, that a feeling of changed circumstances and of the necessity to adapt to the new conditions characterized the settlers' attitudes.

With this section we conclude the analysis of the "middle phase" in Oren's development. The themes presented in the last three chapters were rendered in detail since they are crucial for understanding the course of the village's growth. The rigors of

farming and rural life; the recurrent crises and political squabbles; and the community's highly dependent position are among
the major characteristics of Oren during this period. The villagers' "mood" was typically pessimistic, as they often despaired
of the future. There was little room for romanticism: their life
was harsh and most were displeased with it. Yet, while the difficulties should not be minimized, much was accomplished. Some
of the settlers were mastering the new farm techniques; they
grew more accustomed to and skilled in their relations with public agencies; they took a more active role in directing community affairs; and their ties to one another also deepened. These
gains were almost unnoticed, hidden in the fury of factional dispute or antagonism against the Department. This does not mean
that this period was "necessary"—that without this phase the
program would not have succeeded or that alternatives were not
possible. Rather, it is fair to conclude that during this period the
settlers became more accustomed to their new conditions, so that
in the next phase, as we shall later see, they were able to capital-
ize upon this experience.

CHAPTER VII

Reciprocal Change at Oren

THE dominant approach in the past few chapters has been chronological. Before proceeding to the next phase in Oren's development, however, it will be useful to draw some conclusions regarding one important dimension of Oren's experience: the process and results of culture contact.

As we have seen, the settlers at Oren were predisposed to adopt new behavioral patterns. Indeed, their new circumstances seemed to demand changes in thought and action. A quick review of these circumstances—immigration to Israel, settlement in a cooperative village, a farming career, relationships with a different type of bureaucracy—indicates how truly different their conditions were and leads us to expect that the immigrants adopted new forms of behavior.

This is the now familiar view of "culture change": we expect that immigrants, facing new conditions and in contact with a "receiving society," will adopt new techniques, wear new clothing, or enter into different social relations.[1] This conclusion seems commonplace, and it is supported by many studies of cul-

[1] This point is made repeatedly in the articles contained in W. D. Borrie, *The Cultural Absorption of Immigrants* (Paris, UNESCO, 1959).

ture contact and change.[2] What is less well appreciated,
however, is that culture contact may also provoke important
changes within the receiving society. Not only were the immigrants themselves changed, immigration and settlement also generated changes within the veteran community. Both dimensions
of the contact process—the reciprocal nature of culture contact
—need to be analyzed and appreciated.

The Settlers

Social change among the immigrants may be seen on a number
of different levels. There have been changes in technology, in
social relations, and in their political status. Although these are
related developments, it is best to consider them separately.

The adoption by the settlers of farming materials and skills is a
striking instance of change. There is a large gap indeed between
peddling in a Moroccan market and raising tomatoes in a Negev
village. While, as was earlier pointed out, not all of the settlers
mastered the new skills, they all engaged in farming: seeds and
fertilizers, irrigation and credits, cooperative marketing, and
weeding were part of this new way of life. The villagers worked
in the fields, using tools and techniques that were new and
different from their previous experience. Although the farming
role involved severe status conflicts and many became dissatisfied, all of the settlers used the same materials. The younger settlers might be more successful farmers and members of the kin
groups have advantages, but the community as a whole was engaged in farming.

In addition to these specific farming skills, the settlers' contacts with Israeli society led to an expansion of their cultural in-
ventory. They were prepared—and indeed eager—to accept
technological innovations. For example, only the more affluent

[2] "Culture contact" studies are legion. One sample of this kind is
in E. Spicer, *Human Problems in Technological Change* (New York:
Russell Sage Foundation, 1952).

immigrants came to Israel with radios. Now each home boasted a radio. Many families purchased a gas plate, thereby replacing the older system of cooking on kerosene burners, and some also obtained a refrigerator and washing machine. One group of settlers purchased a tractor, and began to work their fields and the fields of others with the new machine. Most of those who had the financial resources made similar investments; they purchased mechanical equipment or household furnishings. It is important to recognize that the immigrants at Oren wanted what other Israelis had or wanted: they too wished to acquire a car or motor scooter, stylish clothing, and a better radio. Their desires included dairy cattle, a tractor, and other mechanized implements. They no longer took the old country for comparison, but rather looked to the new land for reference. The settlers did not compare their standard of living with Morocco so much as with Tel Aviv and Beersheba.

Obtaining accurate information regarding changes in diet and housing is made difficult by the lack of data on these conditions in Morocco. The settlers themselves related that their diet had not changed substantially: they continued to eat the same foods they ate in Morocco, though in different proportions. They now ate less meat and fish; these were not readily available, and meat was generally expensive. In Israel the villagers ate more *couscous* (a traditional doughy mixture) and more vegetables than previously, because they could not obtain other desired foods. As with farmers the world over, what was plentiful in the field was plentiful on the plate. Some women baked bread several times a week in earthen ovens built near the house; others raised vegetables familiar to their diet which were difficult to obtain in Israel. New foods, by and large, had not been adopted; for example, milk and cheese products, a basic part of the general Israeli diet, had not been widely accepted. The settlers' diet rather lacked variety and became more repetitive.

The village homes were different from the immigrants' former homes in Morocco. The concrete block houses, each of which included two rooms, were probably larger and airier than the dwellings most immigrants lived in in Morocco. The interior arrangements, however, did not easily permit the maintenance of the extended family. Households where parents lived with their married sons were therefore characterized by conflicts. In some cases this problem was partially solved by adding on a ramshackle frame room; the elder parents usually lived there, partly separated from the young couple. This arrangement was far from satisfactory, however, and the problem of joint residence remained a sore issue.

While village life led to the adoption of a new technology and to an expanded range of consumer goods, it had a constricting effect upon the settlers' style of life. The fact that the immigrants now lived in small rural villages had important consequences. It will be recalled that many settlers had previously migrated within Morocco itself; individuals and family groups left small towns and villages and moved to large urban centers. For these migrants, the urban traditions began to be influential, while village traditions became less binding. Many features of urban culture were desired and adopted: movies and the coffee house, the promenade, manufactured goods, and luxury items became part of their new culture complex. These things had important symbolic as well as intrinsic value: they represented the culture of the secular West and embodied a new, desired way of life.

It is ironic that in Israel this urbanizing group was settled in small, rural villages. The cycle of migration had been from Moroccan town or village to Moroccan city, and from there, once more, to village. The irony inheres in the fact that ruralization was based upon a model foreign to the settlers: the ideology of the veteran European pioneers. The founders of the *moshav* movement were city persons, urban intellectuals who self-consciously sought to transform themselves into a peasantry.

The Moroccan immigrants were placed willy-nilly in their path: new city folk had been relocated into villages.

Ruralization resulted in a narrowing of the immigrants' forms of cultural expression. There were few opportunities for them to engage in the activities they had previously learned to value. There was no coffee house at Oren, no place for men to gather and chat. A movie arrived once a week, if at all, and the "theater" was a temporary building, barren of furnishings. There was no one to visit except the neighbors and "no place to go." The desires of urban life were present, but there were few opportunities for attaining them.

Turning next to social relations, there too one discovers extensive changes. In particular, a new system of social status grew dominant, and major changes also took place in primary group relations. How and why these changes occurred may best be seen in the context of Oren's brief history.

Immigration and settlement initiated two complementary processes: social leveling first took place, and new criteria of social differentiation then became effective. It will be recalled that, historically, wealth and ritual position were indices of social status in Morocco: privilege and power were associated with the rabbis and the rich. Age, too, was associated with deference and respect. At Oren, however, these criteria had little meaning. Few immigrants arrived with substantial resources, and those who had capital soon left the village. There was no eminent religious specialist within the group. Moreover, most of the immigrants were strangers, and consequently they had no easily available means of revealing their previous social status. At the same time, the settlement authorities themselves promoted a program of "equalization." The Department officials recognized none of the traditional social distinctions: each settler received the same sized home, everyone was given the same tools and equipment, and all of the immigrants were expected to begin a new life of agricultural labor. An immigrant's previous position made little difference to the village instructors: old and young, the immigrant who had been an independent artisan as well as those who had been poor peddlars, all received equal treatment.

For a brief period, the old prestige symbols remained valid: the first village committee was dominated by older immigrants who had held higher status positions in Morocco. But these traditional symbols were soon brushed aside and replaced by different ones. Facility in Hebrew was the first new status mark. Soon, however, most of the immigrants gained some mastery of the new language. Two other bases of differentiation then grew in importance, and have remained major indices of social status: success in farming and a talent for leadership. Status was accorded to those settlers who successfully adapted to a life of physical labor, as well as those who were able to influence others and manage community affairs.

The emergence of these new prestige symbols resulted both from the demands of the situation and from the conscious efforts of the settlement authorities. The village instructors rewarded those farmers who showed promise: successful men were praised, they developed closer relations with the instructors, and they received greater financial rewards. In addition, those who prospered were admired, however grudgingly, by their fellow immigrants. The bewildering new life, with its strange ways and meanings, also opened avenues for settlers possessing ambition and talent for leadership. The more ambitious sought to gain the support of others. If they were moderate and cooperative, they also enjoyed the instructors' support. On the other hand, leadership might also be grasped by opposing the Department. This fluid situation often meant that the more aggressive settlers seized influential positions.

Social status was formally bestowed by membership on the village committee. When Sephardi and his followers resigned from the committee during Oren's first year, the new elections represented not only a change in leadership, but also validation of the new prestige symbols. The new committee members then elected were drawn from among the successful farmers and more aggressive leaders. These men were, moreover, younger persons: in contrast with the first committee, they were all between the ages of twenty-five and thirty-five, and several were even younger. The older settlers relinquished leadership posts and ambitions. The young, who were physically more able and who better understood the new world, have since dominated the committees.

The new *moshav* situation also affected relations within the family unit and between members of kinship groups. If, prior to immigration, the family was in the midst of a social crisis, then certainly these tensions grew in Israel. Better able to work and quicker to adopt the language and symbols of the new culture, youngsters challenged parental authority. Their enhanced prestige clashed with the traditional norms. The tragedies of immigrant generations were thus repeated: there were painful misunderstandings between father and son, mother and daughter, resulting in nagging tensions. There were also new problems of husband-wife relations, as some women demanded greater independence. The family unit thus experienced continuing tensions: this crisis was unresolved, and in fact became magnified under the immigration and *moshav* conditions.

Unlike the family unit, however, social bonds between kinsmen were often strengthened. The kinship group, a social form that had become disorganized in Morocco, reunited in Israel. In Morocco, migration and urbanization dispersed kinsmen throughout the land and generated social conditions in which kinship ties became lax. Israeli conditions changed this disintegrating trend: the kin group not only reconstituted itself, it also assumed new social functions.

Many new immigrants chose to live with kinsmen: in the new land, under unfamiliar conditions, they sought at least social familiarity. In many instances these were persons who had not previously lived together or who had been separated for many years. Oren, which had initially been a community of unrelated persons, soon became a village in which most persons had some kinsfolk in the community, and the two large kin groups composed nearly half the population.

This type of "chain migration" is a familiar feature of immigration.[3] More unusual, however, is the effect that the *moshav* system had upon the kinship bonds. Within the *moshav* community, kinsmen cooperated with one another: they lived along the same street, worked together in planting or harvesting, and sometimes made joint purchases. These activities forged new links between them. Even more important, kinship assumed a new political dimension; since political control of the village was advantageous, the kin groups became opposed units in the contest for power. The recurrent disputes intensified their interdependence, and these groups became increasingly solidary units. Thus, in effect, not only were kinship groups partially reconstituted, they adopted new social functions and became, in contrast to Moroccan life, more prominent social units.

This change had unanticipated consequences. One of the aims of the Department's directed change program was to build personal relationships upon criteria different from family ties. In a situation where kinship and power were so closely intertwined, however, family ties were decisive rather than relations based upon friendship or age. More universal types of social relations might have been nascent, but they could not prosper under the pressure of kinship obligations. The strengthening of kinship ties therefore restricted the growth of other types of social groups.

Thus far, changes in technology and social relations have been considered. Significant changes also took place in regard to the settlers' political status. Whereas, formerly, the immigrants were Jews in a Muslim-dominated society, in Israel they became mem-

[3] C. A. Price, "Immigration and Group Settlement," in W. D. Borrie, *op. cit.*

bers of the politically dominant Jewish majority. This shift brought a general feeling of security and satisfaction. "I never knew how to raise tomatoes," a settler once remarked. "I never worked in the sun. In Morocco I had a store, and we ate meat each day. But here I feel free. I'm no longer afraid." No matter how integral Jews were to the social system of old Morocco, and no matter how some sought and gained membership in the new Moroccan state, most Jews always lived in a shadow of fear. This was now gone: in their new circumstances they had a sense of security.

Not only did the settlers have a new sense of freedom, they also considered themselves to be participants: they were now Jews in a Jewish State, and consequently they were concerned with Israel's fate and felt themselves to be part of the state's future. The immigrants did not always fully understand national political developments, but they did identify with the state and its problems. Moreover, they developed new expectations regarding the state and the general society. Since the nation was Jewish, they expected its members to act "as Jews"—to behave toward them in a fashion that indicated warmth, sympathy, and assistance. These expectations, however, often led to conflict and disappointment, particularly in the settlers' relations with bureaucrats. For, instead of acting as "Jews," the officials tended to behave as "bureaucrats." Settler-bureaucrat ties were therefore usually tense and not infrequently explosive. In effect, the immigrants were drawn into the total society, but they also encountered some of its rigidities.

Immigration brought new symbols of social identity: if in Morocco the immigrant had been a "Jew," in Israel he became a "Moroccan." In the new society, ethnic origin was a fact of primary significance: every member of the society had an ethnic identity which distinguished him from others. An immigrant was recognized and known by this identity: for one to be Moroccan therefore made a difference. As was earlier pointed out,

the Moroccan immigrants were strongly convinced that they
were discriminated against because they were Moroccans. This
identity was sometimes borne with shame, and it led to under-
tones of tension in social relations. On the other hand, their new
identity made the immigrants part of an ethnic group and
directed contacts to persons who were like themselves. For example, the immigrants often chose the company of fellow Moroccans; those who left Oren for a different *moshav* always
chose another Moroccan community. All of the marriages contracted in Israel by members of the village were between Moroccans. "Being a Moroccan" thus bore overtones of communal-
ity and mutual sympathy: it distinguished the immigrants from
others and drew them closer together.

These various levels of change indicate the scope of the revo-
lution that transformed the settlers' lives. However, there were
also many signs of cultural continuity. Although new farming
methods had been successfully transferred, new cultural traditions were adopted more slowly. There are many examples of
the gap between the settlers' way of life and the new Israeli traditions. Almost all of the male settlers spoke some Hebrew; they
used the language, though they were not fully at ease with it.
Most women, however, knew scarcely any Hebrew; this defi-
ciency handicapped their contacts with other Israelis and limited
their understanding of the new culture. Only three families received a daily Hebrew newspaper; the villagers were only
vaguely aware of events in Israel and the world. While each
home had a radio, the most popular programs were Arab-
language broadcasts from the neighboring countries. None of
the settlers felt themselves to be part of an Israeli movement or
political party; these were largely unknown or considered with
deep cynicism. Most holidays and family events (a birth or marriage) were celebrated in the traditional fashion rather than according to more secular Israeli traditions. As these examples suggest, while there were major technological and social changes,

the immigrants' cultural traditions tended to persist. They undertook new acts with new equipment, but they did not yet adopt new ceremonies or different forms of thought.

Cultural continuity might also be seen in those areas where change appeared to be most marked—in the settlers' farm work. Some settlers, particularly the older ones, approached the farming tasks in a peddler-like fashion. The man who spread less than the required amount of fertilizer or who irrigated for shorter periods of time—all in an effort to save money—in effect approached the soil in a manner analogous to a peddler dealing with customers. He cheated the earth as a peddler might cheat a customer: he provided less than the required amount, since costs were thereby less, and who would know? One dealt with the soil as one dealt previously with clients and merchandise.

The private marketing practices indicated similar continuities. Most settlers, it will be recalled, cultivated small plots of vegetables which they marketed privately. Each Thursday they sold their produce in the weekly Beersheba market. This practice was strikingly reminiscent of peddling in Morocco. Many brought their sacks to town by wagon, thereby saving the cost of motor transportation; they left Oren late on Wednesday night, arrived in town before dawn, and arranged their wares in the vegetable market. There they rented a scale, and squatting behind their goods and calling out a price, sold their wares to the local Jewish and Bedouin customers. This practice was another instance of the continuation of the peddler tradition.

This type of response to changed circumstances extended to still other areas. The health clinic established near Oren was visited regularly by the settlers. Whenever the doctor arrived, long lines formed as persons waited for treatment. Vaccinations, medications, and hospitalization were familiar aspects of the treatment of disease. Yet, many settlers also availed themselves of the more traditional medical practitioners: the village rabbi and a local rabbi-healer. When a baby was ill he was brought to the clinic, but he wore an amulet around his neck. If a man had mysterious pains he consulted the doctor, but he was also likely to go to the local rabbi-healer, who found the cause and cure of disease in traditional cabalistic lore. Most persons said they were not superstitious and that the traditional techniques were old-fashioned. Yet these same people turned to the old practitioners for help and continued to understand disease in traditional terms. In this instance, the new techniques were readily accepted, but the older ones were maintained along with them.

While continuity in thought and tradition characterized the village as a whole, some settlers did adopt the new cultural patterns and took on Israeli traditions. This was particularly true of those young immigrants who underwent prolonged resocializing experiences in the army or other educational settings. These young men and women exhibited many signs of acculturation. The number of such cases at Oren was limited: two of the boys were in *aliyat noar* groups, and six served in the army. Yet the experience of this small group suggests a paradoxical conclusion: precisely those who changed most tended to leave the village. Four of the six who served in the army left, and only one of the two *aliyat noar* trainees remained. A youth who served in the army had difficulty readjusting to his family and village. To whatever degree he had taken on new attitudes and expectations, he was not well understood by his family and former friends: he had changed while the others had not. The returnee was not only under pressure at home, he also longingly recalled the life he experienced away from home. In the village he searched for others like himself, for friends who would understand him. If the returnee did not find support in the village, he was likely to leave; most often he went to the city, where he might find a more satisfying life. It was thus the least acculturated, the most traditional among the settlers, who remained in the village. Those persons whom the instructors and the Department considered most suitable candidates for leadership were therefore lost to the community. Paradoxically, success in the resocialization program did not necessarily lead to an acculturated village.

There are, of course, variations on this theme. Some returnees did accommodate themselves to the village. Back in the old familiar setting, among family and kin, they reverted to traditional norms of behavior. They lived between two cultural worlds: the old culture of their parents and family, and the new Israeli way of life. Within the village they moved between their parents' home and the home of the instructors. Generally speaking, they were ill at ease in both places: they might reject their home, but they were not fully accepted by the Israeli instructors. These young people were marginal persons, expressing all the classic tensions of marginality. Discontent and ill at ease, they became candidates for departure.

In summary, the settlers' Israeli experience surely resulted in far-ranging changes. The changes moved at different rates, however: a new technology was adopted, but older cultural traditions persisted. The settlers' patterns of social relations were altered, and their way of life shifted; yet they remained distinctively Moroccan. This identity seemed likely to persist for some time in the future. Further changes in social relations, or in consumer styles, might occur, but the settlers, living in a small, rural community, would probably retain their distinctively ethnic way of life.

The Veteran Society

Culture contact is a reciprocal process: all of the groups in contact may become changed. How then did the Moroccan immigrants influence the veterans?

Contact was selective, restrictive—only some of the members of the two groups interacted and then only in certain social contexts. The context of contact was the *moshav*, and although they established casual contacts with many persons, the settlers' most direct, abiding relations were with members of the Settlement Department. It was within these two spheres—the *moshav* and the settlement system—that reciprocal change can best be seen. The Oren experience illustrates how an immigrant group reshaped and induced changes within important institutions of a receiving society.

How did the Moroccan settlers respond to the *moshav?* This cooperative format was imposed upon them, *and yet they, in turn, reinterpreted the* moshav *system.* Reinterpretation—"the process by which old meanings are ascribed to new elements, or by which new values change the cultural significance of old forms" [4]—was well illustrated at Oren. Although the village instructors sought to cast the *moshav* ideals upon the settlers, quite the reverse process occurred: the settlers changed the *moshav* system to accord with their own ideals.

Different features of traditional *moshav* life were reinterpreted. For example, the villagers' translation of the *moshav* concept of equality differed significantly from the classic definition. For the founders of the *moshav*, equality meant equal opportunities—every member of the community was to receive the same chance. At Oren, however, equality was usually translated to mean equal shares and, in fact, tended to approach leveling. It was not so much that people were to have equal opportunities as that resources were to be divided into equal portions. To cite several instances of this ideal in practice, the settlers would insist upon an equal distribution of monthly loans regardless of the conditions of the crops. Their insistence upon equal distribution meant that the Settlement Department was often unable to fully implement its program of rewarding the more successful settlers: the villagers resisted programs that tended away from automatic, equal division. To take another example, when a teacher's helper was needed in the village nursery school,

[4] M. Herskovits, *Cultural Anthropology* (New York: Knopf, 1955), p. 492.

several teen-age girls submitted applications for the job. In order to appease the insistence on equality, pressure was exerted for a rotation system, in which each of the girls would work for several weeks (to the confusion of the children) and the remuneration would be equally divided.

A similar process of reinterpretation took place in regard to the *moshav* principle of cooperation. In theory, cooperation in the *moshav* was to be practiced among all of the village members. At Oren, however, cooperation did not join all men, but rather kinsmen. Each group of kin was a relatively closed unit, and mutual aid was restricted to the group itself. Primary group solidarity was dominant, and village-wide cooperation existed only on a formal level. The formal community cooperative structure was also changed. As was earlier pointed out, cooperative marketing only partially existed: the settlers did not have an ideology of cooperation, and they felt no twinge of conscience when they marketed their goods privately. Quite the opposite was in fact true: they looked forward to the weekly trip to market, where they sold their goods and made purchases in a traditional fashion. That this practice was considered illegal, or that it placed strain upon the *moshav* system, did not in any way deter the tendency toward individual marketing; the settlers continued to find private channels. Here again, the settlers' cultural ideals altered the *moshav* system.

Similar tendencies may be observed in relation to the traditional *moshav* antagonism to exploitation. There was no abhorrence of exploitation among the settlers at Oren: they had no ideological compunctions against hiring labor. On the contrary. Whenever possible, workers were hired to perform the more menial farm tasks. They were usually young boys or girls from a neighboring town who appeared each day in search of work. They were hired at low wage rates and assigned to pick or cultivate. Hiring labor had also become common practice in many

older *moshavim;* yet in those communities it was not usually entered into so freely. (In the older villages, hired workers were
usually paid a relatively high union salary.)

The settlers' values also led to a reorganization of the
moshav's political structure. In contrast with the original
moshavim, the women at Oren never attended community meetings. There was, therefore, neither universal representation nor
universal choice. The settlers' values in regard to male-female
roles limited participation in community political life. Moreover,
election and choice were not normally based upon universalistic
criteria, but rather on particularistic affiliations. Voting tended
to follow family lines: the settlers inevitably supported their
kinsmen, and democracy in this instance meant that the largest
bloc of kin dominated the political scene. It is not that merit and
ability were not recognized, but rather that these qualities alone
were insufficient and therefore had to be set within more familiar terms, the bonds of kinship. In place of open choice there
were solidary factions, and instead of policy decision there were
rival group jealousies.

Finally, the *moshav* stress upon independence was reinterpreted within Oren. The *moshav* way of life was designed to
foster individual freedom: each member was to be independent,
a man who thought and acted as a proud producer. Life at Oren,
however, was intrinsically dependent, and the villagers' old sense
of dependence became strengthened. Many awaited and indeed
demanded outside guidance and decision; they were prepared to
accept the exertions of others and even to demand more. This
old cultural ideal was strengthened in the new situation, and the
reinforcement in turn affected the entire settlement experiment.
This far-reaching change sharply differentiated Oren and villages like it from the older, classic *moshavim.*

These examples indicate some of the areas in which reinterpretation took place. Set within the *moshav* organizational framework, required to function within a cooperative system, the

settlers at Oren reacted to the new situation in terms of their own traditions. Oren was not a duplicate of the original *moshavim* upon which it was modeled. The settlers who were placed within a framework in order to be changed by it changed the framework instead. Oren resembled the classic *moshav* in plan and appearance but not in thought and deed.

Reinterpretation represented one type of change resulting from the contact situation—a change in the receiving society's social forms. There were additional dimensions to this reciprocal process. Culture contact led to organizational and behavioral changes within the Settlement Department bureaucracy. While this change was of a different order than the reinterpretation of the *moshav*, it too stemmed from the new conditions created by immigration and settlement.

Changes within the Settlement Department may be termed institutional adjustments. Institutional adjustment refers to the process by which members of formally organized groups consciously or unconsciously redefine their tasks and assume new roles in order to adjust to new social conditions. For example, contact conditions may result in new types of status and authority relations, as well as in new definitions and expressions of institutional tasks. Various forms of internal reorganization may also occur. This process is well illustrated in the Oren case: contact with immigrants led to redefinitions in the settlement system and thereby altered the status position and role behavior of the Department personnel.

Relations between the Department and its settler clients began changing with the advent of mass immigration. Historically, the Department's activity in directing settlement was restricted to loaning capital and extending expert agricultural advice to groups of pioneer farmers. The Department extended long-term capital loans, and the villages retained a large degree of autonomy in directing their own socioeconomic development. Department experts acted in an advisory capacity, but a village's investment program was primarily the settlers' own concern. At Oren, however, as well as in other immigrant villages, the Department's financial relationship with the settlers became completely reorganized. Rather than simply dispensing capital, the Department retained ownership and effective control over much of its capital investment. It no longer acted merely as a supply agency but planned and directed how its capital was to be used.

Loans or equipment were not granted to the settlers, but rather leased to them. Each individual settler was required to sign a contract to the effect that the equipment and installations he received were given on lease and that they remained the property of the Department. Settlement Department officials described this new relationship in the following terms:

All the investments made by the Department in the villages are given for the utilization of the candidate for settlement (as licensee) until he reaches a position of consolidation and is ratified as a permanent settler in the village. The candidate will be entitled to utilize this property so long as permission has not been revoked by the Department. The status of the settler throughout his period of candidacy is that of a licensee, who is permitted to utilize Department property to cultivate and develop his farm in accordance with the plan determined by the Department.[5]

Thus, the horse and cart allotted by the Department was Department property; the settler might use the equipment, but he was not permitted to sell or exchange it. Were he to sell the horse he would be liable to prosecution in the courts. Similar contracts were entered into with regard to homes, farm buildings, agricultural equipment, and the like. (A settler who left the village was responsible for paying rent for the period during which he lived in the home allotted to him.) The "position of consolidation" described in the quoted passage refers to the period following

[5] "The Agricultural Settlement Department," *Report of the 25th World Zionist Congress* (in Hebrew) (Jerusalem: Jewish Agency, 1955), p. 21.

completion of the investments planned by the Department: a village became "consolidated" when the villagers received the capital necessary for them to become self-sustaining. Neither Oren nor any of the other new *moshavim* in the Negev area had yet reached this stage. They continued to receive various forms of capital investment from the Department and were not yet responsible for repaying these loans.

This new type of contract completely changed the traditional Department-settler relationship. Whereas the village as a unit had formerly been the contracting agent, each individual settler now became directly responsible for the capital he received. The Department retained ownership over the capital; the villagers were licensees who might "utilize this property so long as permission has not been revoked by the Department." It is hardly surprising that the "owner" then became increasingly concerned with directing the efficient use of his capital: the settler "is permitted to utilize Department property to cultivate and develop his farm *in accordance with the plan determined by the Department.*" (Italics mine.) How each individual settler used the capital became the Department's main concern; each settler was required to follow the Settlement Department's instructions or face the threat of losing further support. As is apparent, no matter how benevolent its policies were, the Department increasingly assumed the position of landlord, and the settlers the position of tenants.

Why did this new relationship emerge? Until approximately 1952, the traditional Department-settler contract had been maintained: although instructors were attached to the new *moshavim* as management experts, in these villages the Department simply made allocations of funds and equipment to the community. Local village committees who received the capital directed its distribution. This program soon met with serious difficulties in the new villages. Since these communities were formed administratively, the settlers lacked any kind of ties to the *moshav* sys-

tem and its ideology. It was therefore not uncommon for settlers
to dispose of the materials allotted to them (by sale or trade),
pocket the money, and later use it for private purposes. Department personnel found themselves in a position in which they
were channeling large sums of money into the villages, only to
have these sums rapidly vanish. Furthermore, the new villages
could not carry the burden of debts incurred by individual settlers who borrowed large amounts and then could not, or would
not, make repayment. Village debts often grew to astronomical
sums without there being any real possibility of repayment. In
order to guarantee its investment, the Department therefore
adopted an individual contract-type program: since the village
could not be responsible for its members, each individual settler
would guarantee the capital leased to him. While the reasons for
this shift may seem apparent, the implications were far-reaching:
these contracts not only lent a formal, legalistic tone to villager-
Department relations, they also redefined the relationship in a
new and fundamentally different manner.

This new type of relationship was strengthened by the Department's policy of extending monthly loans. Since the settlers
lacked funds for purchasing consumer goods, the Department
lent the villagers small amounts each month. Collateral for the
loans was the crops the settlers planted and tended. Once having
extended these loans, the Department needed to devise procedures whereby it might protect its investment. Department
workers were therefore concerned not only with how the settler
maintained the original capital investment—homes, livestock, irrigation equipment, and the like—but also with each individual's
daily work. A villager who farmed inefficiently or who marketed his produce privately was seen to be haphazardly or il-
legally utilizing the extended capital. In this fashion, the Department's range of interest and control became much wider: it saw
its role as directing the settlers' daily work, thereby guaranteeing its agricultural investments. Crops growing in the settlers'

fields were the Department's property: Department officials who inspected the rows of sugar beets or tomatoes were, in effect, inspecting crops that in large measure belonged to them. However reasonable they may seem, these policies only served to strengthen the landlord-tenant contract: the villagers became lessees, working the land and tending the crops.

These changes were further accompanied by shifts in status positions. Whereas high status had been traditionally accorded to the pioneer settlers, at Oren the officials rather than the farmers held the elite positions. There are various reasons for this change in status. For one thing, cultural differences between the groups lent the officials a higher position: Department workers were recognized and admired as models of the new and desirable Israeli way of life. Moreover, the Department personnel obviously had wide areas of direct authority. Village instructors or district executives were entrusted with making decisions that influenced the settlers' fate and future. The settlers' position also changed, since they had only limited means of influencing policy decisions. Groups of pioneer settlers had direct lines of communication to the highest levels of policy making. The immigrants, however, had no such contacts. They influenced plans by resistance and demonstrations, rather than by participating in the process of policy formation.

Another indication of change was the new kind of penalties employed by the settlement authorities. In disputes with pioneer-type settlers the Department normally coaxed, argued, and sought to convince the settlers of the validity of its programs. These efforts might be unsuccessful, and the villagers, who had other channels to authority, might proceed to develop their own plans and programs. At Oren, however, the Department brought severe economic pressure to bear upon uncooperative settlers. Those who did not follow Department crop programs were punished by not being granted full credits; uncooperative villagers often did not receive commodities that were generally distributed throughout the village. Those who acted in an illegal fashion were even prosecuted in court: the Department could bring suits against villagers who sold their produce privately and did not return loans granted to them, or who sold or otherwise disposed of capital goods distributed to them. Relations between the two groups thus assumed a formal, legalistic basis: while warm personal ties might develop between certain officials and the villagers, their contacts were framed within an increasingly formal system.

The mass settlement program initiated an entire new series of roles for Department personnel. "Village instructor" or "farm manager" were novel designations; an entirely new bureaucratic hierarchy was quickly developed. These were new positions, and their behavioral definitions were usually very imprecise. Village instructors were uncertain whether they were teachers or managers: should they be receptive to the villagers' demands or serve the Department's interests? Not only did ambiguity in role definition lead to uncertainty on the part of the Department personnel, but an instructor or District head was often thrust into a situation for which he was hardly prepared. Villagers sometimes turned to a young instructor and requested him to act as a judge in a family dispute. Agricultural instructors advised immigrants regarding their intimate personal problems, and farm managers began functioning as social workers. Thus it is fair to conclude that it was not only the immigrants who adopted new roles; the receiving personnel assumed equally novel roles.

What caused these changes to take place? Why did the Department reformulate its traditional policies, and why have the administrators and their clients adopted new roles? One interpretation might be to view these developments as stemming from internal bureaucratic forces: the tendency of the Department, in seeking to expand its scope of control, to reformulate and extend its usual policies. Such an interpretation would emphasize forces within the bureaucracy itself—a kind of

Parkinson's Law—rather than the contact conditions. This interpretation is not, however, supported by an examination of Department relations with new, veteran settlements. That is, in its dealings with pioneer-type settlers—members of new *kibbutzim*, for example—the Department maintained its traditional relationships: although in recent years Department planners took a greater role in guiding these latter villages, higher status continued to be associated with the veteran settlers, and ties between administrators and clients were typically informal and highly personal. It would therefore appear that changes within the Department arose chiefly out of the new contact conditions. Faced with the problem of settling untrained, nonselected immigrants in cooperative farming villages, the Department adjusted its policies and entered into new types of relations. The new landlord role grew from the attempt to adapt to new social conditions— the attempt to settle Moroccan immigrants in a Negev *moshav*. Had the settlers at Oren been "pioneers," then the usual relations would have applied; but since they were "reluctant pioneers," their contacts with Department officials led to widespread changes in the normal policies and practices.

Changes similar to those described in this chapter took place within other veteran institutions. For example, the Jewish Agency Absorption Department and the Histadruth (the labor federation) also adopted new and different modes for dealing with their clients. In these and other cases the informal, personalized relationships were replaced by more rigid, bureaucratized procedures. As with the Department, new roles were adopted by administrators and officials of these groups. The processes of change that were described for the Department had therefore a general relevance throughout the veteran society as a whole.

What this analysis illustrates, then, is the reciprocal character of culture contact—the fact that different types of change derive from the contacts between diverse groups. It is important to emphasize that the types of change are different. The problem is not to see that while one group—in this case, the Moroccan settlers—adopted the veterans' technology, the veterans did not make similar adaptations. This is the familiar view, a view that concludes inevitably that culture change is a one-way process, since new materials do not flow equally in both directions. Rather, the advantage of the reciprocal view is precisely to see that contacts result in changes on different levels. For example, trait adoption is surely very different from institutional adjustment: the former is a type of change resulting from copying or modeling newly available forms, while the latter arises from decisions made due to new situations. Furthermore, institutional adjustment is a reversible kind of change: a group such as the Department may enter into different types of relations with its clients rather freely. Changes in primary group relations, on the other hand, are the products of much more complex historical factors and are not easily reversible. No matter how different these changes may be, however, they have in common the fact that they derive from the culture contact situation. Studying culture contact on different levels—viewing it as a reciprocal process—thus uncovers the varieties of change that contact provokes.

CHAPTER VIII

The Development Process:
A Comparative Perspective

EARLY in 1960, following prolonged debate, the Settlement Department introduced several reforms in Oren's cooperative credit practices. At first experimentally, and then more whole-heartedly, credits were extended to each individual villager rather than to the village committee or other communal body for distribution. While it is difficult to sort out and identify a key event in a community's history, this change does seem to have had profound impact upon the village's subsequent growth. (It was introduced in some eighty other new *moshavim* at the same time.) This fundamental reform, redefining as it did the conditions of village life, marks off the third phase in the village's brief history.

It will be helpful to review briefly the previous credit practices. The original system, it will be recalled, was cooperative rather then individual: the village as a unit received credits or capital grants, and these were then allotted to the individual settlers according to decisions made by village authorities (the village committee and Department personnel). Since loans were centralized and granted to the village as a whole, the cooperative ties were consequently great: how each settler used his credits affected all of the others. It will also be recalled that monthly subsistence loans were granted to each settler; the size of these loans was fixed by the Department, and they were to be repaid following the harvest. Earlier, we saw how these cooperative arrangements had become a source of misunderstanding and conflict. For example, in Chapters IV and V incidents were related which indicated how errors and inefficient management led to friction between groups of settlers or between the village and the Department; the illegal private marketing practices had similar results. This system was a major cause of conflict and dissatisfaction.

Two steps were taken to reform the credit system. First, mechanical changes were introduced in the water supply system so that each individual settler could be billed for the amount of water he used. (The pipes were rearranged in a manner such that the flow of water could be cut off on one line without disturbing the supply elsewhere.) Water bills had previously been paid by the village as a whole; the village instructor or secretary paid the bill from whatever funds were then at the village's disposal. Since the funds available were not drawn equally from all of the settlers—the successful farmers contributed a larger proportion—this meant that the successful farmers in effect paid the bills of those who were less efficient. As was noted earlier, this arrangement often led to private marketing and to the chain of complications that followed. Furthermore, if the village could not pay its water bills, the entire water supply was cut off; both those who could pay their bills and those who could not suffered equally. The 1960 reforms were designed to put an end to this situation. Each settler received a monthly water bill and was required to pay the full amount; payment was made directly, not through the village. If a villager failed to pay his bill, water was turned off on his plot only, without affecting delivery to the entire village. Each settler became directly responsible for meeting his water bill.

These reforms were based on the assumption that the settlers would have funds at their disposal to make periodic payments. Previously, when the village made joint payments, the producers themselves were not concerned with paying monthly bills; the village simply used whatever funds were then available. The change in water supply necessitated reforms in the entire system of credit. Therefore, along with the new water program, a general financial reorganization took place. Instead of granting monthly subsistence loans to each settler, the Department made credit available to each individual at the outset of the crop season. According to this scheme, each farmer could receive the same maximum amount. The size of the loan was based upon a Department estimate of the funds needed to carry out the planting schedule (that is, the costs of seed, fertilizer, tractor, water, and so forth). Although the money loaned was Department capital, the program itself was administered by a regional producers' cooperative; the Department hoped in this way to escape the problems related to banking. At first, these loans were made in a kind of scrip—coupons that could be exchanged only for agricultural commodities. Later, however, cash loans were advanced.

What is significant about these loans is that they were made directly to the individual, without the village or other intermediary acting between borrower and creditor. Each villager signed promissory notes guaranteeing to repay the loans at the close of the crop season; the notes were also signed by two other villagers who acted as guarantors. (Without guarantors a settler could not receive a loan.) At harvest time, the villagers received payment for their crops directly and later repaid their loans. Moreover, according to this plan a settler could sell his crops as he saw fit, either to Tnuva or to private merchants. This new credit arrangement meant that several times each year a settler

signed notes in return for loans and returned the loans at the end
of the crop season. If the loans were not repaid, new credits were
not extended. Generally speaking, however, the cooperative followed a liberal credit policy; new loans were granted if a portion
of the debt was repaid or if natural causes (such as pests) were
responsible for the settler's failure.

There is convincing evidence that this reform had an energiz-
ing effect upon the entire community. The settlers themselves
are of this opinion and so are the planners. For the larger
producers—the more successful farmers—the new system was
an immediate spur to increased activity. These men had always
been opposed to the earlier system whereby their profits were
used to pay the debts of the entire village; they saw the new arrangement as more just and efficient. Many of the others were
also pleased by the reform; they too wanted to receive the fruits
of their work directly. In this system it no longer made any
difference if a villager sold his produce cooperatively or if he
marketed it privately; what was important was that he repaid his
debts. This greater opportunity to speculate—to sell one's crops
to the highest bidder—was keenly appreciated.

Many were pleased by the more direct responsibility they
were given. They had never been fully satisfied with the earlier
arrangement in which their income was determined by the committee's decisions; they saw it as a clumsy system, too open to
favoritism and strife. The basis for earnings was now clear.
"Whoever works gets his money, and if you don't work, then
you don't get anything. It's a harder way, but I prefer it." So
commented one of the settlers; many others echoed his sentiments.

There were some, however, who opposed the change. For the
unsuccessful farmers—those who had not mastered the new
skills or who were displeased with *moshav* life—the new system
came as a harsh blow. These settlers had formerly been guaranteed a monthly income: for political as well as social reasons the

committee had granted them loans regularly. Now, however, their income was fixed by their productivity: if they failed to repay loans they might not receive additional credits. In one case, a settler's water supply was turned off after he had failed to pay his water bill. When this occurred, the others expressed their sympathy and concern, but no one seriously considered returning to the earlier system of total cooperation.

The reforms were thus well received; indeed, they were enthusiastically welcomed. These positive attitudes were soon carried over into behavior. The villagers turned to their farm chores with much greater interest and energy. Both the instructors and the villagers themselves related that they began to work harder and more efficiently. "There isn't a meter of land that isn't being tended," the instructors reported. The land parcels themselves were extended: late in 1960 the Department installed irrigation networks in a previously uncultivated zone, and the area allotted each farmer was increased from twenty-two to thirty-two *dunam* (from five and a half to eight acres). A year later a village orange grove was planted, and each settler received a five-*dunam* (one and a quarter acre) section of the grove. This larger acreage was immediately exploited. The instructors were no longer forced to pressure the settlers into tending their crops; most set their own pace and attended to their chores. They had become more accustomed to the basic farm tasks—planting, fertilizing, weeding, irrigating—and they began to pay closer attention to newer techniques and more efficient work procedures. By that time, the settlers had also learned to distinguish between the more and less remunerative crops. Thus, many preferred vegetable growing, where there was an element of speculation and quick profit, rather than industrial crops. Since they were able to market their crops as they chose, they could take advantage of occasional peaks in vegetable prices. The main crops cultivated in the village became tomatoes, onions, potatoes, and sugar beets; the settlers also grew small

quantities of cucumbers, celery, artichokes, and other vegetables. Cotton and peanuts, two former staples in the crop rotation, were largely eliminated: experience showed that these
crops were not sufficiently profitable. This shift has interesting
implications. Vegetables are sensitive crops, and they demand
constant care. The fact that the settlers chose to plant them indicates that they were prepared to expend long hours in meticu-
lous work. It also suggests that they had begun to master the
farm skills.

Although 1960 and 1961 were drought years in the Negev,
and irrigation costs were increased, agricultural prices tended to
be high. This was particularly true of vegetable prices, which
remained at a premium level. Thus, not only were the settlers
working harder and more efficiently, they were also realizing
greater profits. It was difficult to obtain fully accurate information regarding family incomes. (Since marketing was no longer
under village control, profits were known only to the settlers
themselves and were closely guarded secrets.) The best estimate,
however, is an average family income of approximately I £4,000.
Twelve families were thought to have earned upwards of
I £6,000; on the other hand, eight families apparently had an income of less than I £3,000. In general, however, incomes rose
considerably.

Increased income led, in turn, to greater expenditures in a
wide range of new consumer and production goods. After 1959,
forty-two settlers installed gas cooking facilities in their homes.
Twenty-seven villagers purchased refrigerators. (These figures
are striking when compared with 1959: in that year, one settler
had a gas plate, and none owned a refrigerator.) Seven settlers
installed hot water systems in their homes. There is no evidence
to indicate that these purchases were made possible by reducing
other expenses; settlers purchased refrigerators not by limiting
their food budget, but rather as a result of a generally higher
standard of living. Investments in agricultural machinery were

also made. For example, fifteen settlers purchased their own shoulder sprays for spraying and dusting crops. Even more striking is the purchase of tractors: in 1961 seven tractors were owned and operated by four different groups of settlers. Those who bought tractors used them to work their own land and also rented them to others. One settler purchased (and later sold) a small delivery truck; more recently, a group of villagers bought a large diesel-powered truck which carried produce to market. These settlers were not affluent, yet they had certainly attained a higher standard of living. Moreover, investments in equipment indicated the sense of permanence that was becoming prevalent. The settlers began to see some future in their lives as farmers.

Thus far, we have seen how changes in the credit system lent greater impetus and incentive to farming. The reforms had the additional effect of muting factional strife. The main focus of factional conflict—the Levi-Dehan struggle—had centered around control of the village's political system. Control of the committee was the key to village dominance and economic advantage. However, in the new system of direct credits the committee's responsibility was greatly diminished. Funds were no longer distributed by the committee: committee members did not determine how large the monthly loans would be or the post-harvest percentage of profit each settler would receive. These activities had been the core of the committee's work, and once removed from the realm of group decision, the committee's importance quickly decreased. Problems of community-wide social activities or the village tax rate became topics at committee meetings; these issues were not nearly as fundamental as those which had previously been considered. Indeed, the committee met only infrequently. Being a member of the committee still lent the members high status, but it no longer gave them great power.

Given this new set of conditions, there were fewer overt reasons for factional strife. The Levis and Dehans had less to contest: struggle to control the committee was pointless in a situation where the committee no longer had much power. Members of the two groups maintained internal cooperation, and they continued to support each other's interests: the kin groups continued to be solidary units. Nevertheless, they also arrived at a mutual accommodation. Moshe Dehan was re-elected to the post of village secretary. When the village manager left Oren later, Dehan became responsible for marketing the industrial crops, representing the village to outside groups, making credit arrangements, and so forth. Committee elections were held once each year: membership consisted of individuals from both factions, with the addition of several "neutrals." Neither faction attempted to displace the other—the Levis did not demand the post of village secretary, nor did the Dehans seek to deny the Levis positions on the committee. Indeed, the new political adjustment was reinforced by joint economic ventures. The Levis had purchased a tractor in 1959. A year later the Dehans bought a tractor. For a time both groups competed for work in the fields. Eventually, however, they joined forces in a partnership and shared the work between them. In this fashion they were bound to one another in daily, tangible economic enterprise. Hostility between group members seems to have diminished as cooperative activities enlarged. Both Levi and Dehan family members behaved as if their quarrels had ended; instead of competing, they voiced admiration at one another's accomplishments. Other settlers were skeptical regarding the new alliance: they felt that future clashes of interest were inevitable. Meanwhile, however, the shift in policy led to a muting of factional disputes and a trend toward greater intergroup cooperation.

At one point, however, it did appear as if new disputes would force a change in the village's composition. The cause of this crisis was external in origin: conflicts within the larger Israeli social structure divided the community. National elections were held in 1961. Contrary to the usual procedure, the Levis supported opponents of the political party with which Oren was affiliated. They were actively engaged in this contest, and they sought to persuade the other villagers to support their favorites. Some Department officials, as well as officers of the settlement movement, took the position that the Levis should leave Oren; since the village was associated with one political party, that group's opponents could not be permitted to organize an opposition group within the village itself. During the height of the election campaign, considerable pressure was placed upon the Levis to leave. However, although they apparently did vote for the party of their choice (their favorites received about a quarter of the number of votes cast in the village), passions subsided after the election, and the Levis remained. Once the heat of the election campaign had passed, the issue was largely forgotten.

In addition to these developments—the heightened pace of agricultural activity and the virtual truce between village factions—another important change occurred. After 1960, the villagers themselves assumed greater responsibility for directing community affairs. In July, 1960, Oren's farm manager left the village; he had served for more than two years, and he left to take a position in a neighboring town. The Department at first sought to replace him with another instructor but later decided against sending a *madrich* to the village. Soon thereafter, one of the agricultural instructors also left; for a brief time he was replaced, but the new man also left and was not replaced. Thus, in 1961 only one instructor was assigned to Oren, and his responsibility was restricted to purely technical matters. For the first time since its formation in 1954, there was no manager in the village. The village secretary and the committee became responsible for directing Oren's communal affairs. The secretary, rather than the manager, met with the Department's regional representatives to discuss village issues and make policy decisions. The Department did continue to maintain a directing influence, however: it still held title to village property, directed village investments, and made acreage or production allotments. Changes in housing or the investment rate needed Department approval. Important aspects of the settler-Department relationship were therefore maintained. On the other hand, the organizational system functioned more smoothly, and community crises were less frequent.

If we pause to reflect upon these events—the advances in farming, tendencies toward intergroup cooperation, the relative success in the system of administration—the village's growth in this third phase is surely impressive. In comparison with the previous four or five years, Oren seemed well on the way to becoming a stable, viable community. This conclusion does not mean that all conflicts had become resolved or that a mood of happiness prevailed; not all of the settlers were equally adjusted to farming, and others were jealous of the gains that some were making. The village was increasingly divided between "haves" and "have-nots," and, in the future, this division might grow into sharp conflict. Still, many agreed that their situation had improved, that they had reached a new, more satisfying state in their life in Israel.

This new course has been attributed to the Department's revision of its credit policies. The new credit system does seem to have been the spur to Oren's recent climb. There are important lessons to be learned from this analysis. The turn of events illustrates once again the delicate nature of administered communities; changes in policy have an immediate, direct effect upon village life. It can also be seen that under these circumstances, village development depends upon a choice of programs that blend with the villagers' interests: factional disputes dissolved when the villagers were able to market as they pleased, and the settlers worked more intensively when the cooperative bonds were minimized. Other factors further contributed to the village's growth toward stability. The favorable price structure that prevailed during 1960–1961 assisted the program's success: had the settlers failed to profit from their work, it is unlikely that the reforms would have had the same significance. To be sure, it was preferable to be able to speculate, but only when substantial profits could be made. This fortunate coupling of appropriate administrative reforms with favorable market conditions no doubt contributed to the program's success.

Furthermore, the settlers had become better attuned to farming and *moshav* life. Selective migration had resulted in a majority of settlers who were better adjusted to *moshav* conditions. Some of those who had been disgruntled or who were failing economically had left the village, and while not all of those who remained were successful or pleased with their lot, the more extreme cases had migrated. Migration from Oren virtually ceased by 1960: between 1955 and 1957 sixteen families left the village, while in the period between 1958 and 1962 only three families migrated. Four new families joined the village during the latter period: two of the new members were sons of settlers, and the other two were young immigrants who came to join kinsmen. This population stability indicated that most of the settlers were choosing to remain: they had grown accustomed to the village, were more adept at farming, their incomes had risen, and they were directing their own affairs. In comparison with the earlier years, and also in comparison with what they knew of life outside the village, these were all gratifying achievements. One of the settlers—an older man who had often seemed on the verge of leaving—summarized well the feelings that many had. "We know now what Israel is like. I have my home here, and I know the village and the people. And they know me too. What would I do if I went to town—go to the Labor Exchange each day and wait for work? No, here I'm my own boss." Similar sentiments were voiced by others. For better or for worse—and one could hope for better—Oren had become their home.

This analysis of the third period has not presented as extensive a recording of events as for the first two periods. (I was not residing in the village at that time, so it was not possible to follow the daily course of events.) It may therefore seem as if the documentation is overweighted for the earlier periods, and that this third, "blossoming," stage is relatively out of proportion. Although the presentation of the 1960–1962 phase has been brief, it does show the changed character of the community, as well as the conditions from which these changes derived. The purpose of the analysis has not been to dramatize the difficult early periods, nor to emphasize the village's later apparent greater success. Instead, the objective has been to explain how and why, during an eight year period, Oren grew from relative disorganization and disaffection to a state of greater coherence and viability. The recording of a third stage does indicate some of the bases of this development process.

This chronological examination, emphasizing the villagers' response to Department-initiated reforms, can, however, only partially explain the reasons for Oren's growth. On the basis of this analysis alone, one might assume that all villages in which reforms in the credit system were introduced would follow the same path. To put it differently, the logic of the argument thus far unfolded leads to the conclusion that administrative reforms are the major variable in the development of villages of this type. An examination of other villages in which the same reforms were introduced would not, however, support this conclusion. While some of these villages have prospered, others have not responded to reforms in the credit system, or, for that matter, to other kinds of new policy. Not all immigrant villages followed Oren's course; by 1962, some had become viable communities while others had not.

Tracing the stages in Oren's growth therefore explains the village's development only in part. In order to complete the analysis, it is necessary to inquire if features of Oren's social and political organization were particularly favorable for the community's success. That is, what internal social features, in addition to externally induced administrative reforms, need to be accounted for in explaining Oren's development?

Identifying these factors necessitates the introduction of additional comparative material. This comparison, to which the next portion of this chapter is devoted, emphasizes three variables: the social origins of the settlers, their primary group networks, and their factional alignments. The problem is to determine how these variables influenced the course of village development. Some of the data for the comparison were presented in earlier chapters, where Oren and Shikma were compared along these lines. Data drawn from studies of other Moroccan villages will also be introduced. Although the analysis is preliminary and tentative, it does assist in locating some internal factors promoting village growth.

The comparison between Oren and Shikma is especially useful, since a number of key variables may be controlled. The two villages border upon one another, thereby sharing the same physical setting. The crop program is identical in both villages: members of the two communities received the same sized parcels of land and grow the same crops. Both villages were formed and settled at about the same period, and most of the settlers have lived in Israel for approximately the same length of time. Nearly all of the settlers in the two villages came from Morocco (there were two families of Tunisian immigrants at Oren). Yet, with these features in common, the two adjacent villages developed in very different ways: while Oren progressed to a condition of relative stability and economic growth, Shikma was still characterized by internal crises and minimal agricultural development. Comparing the two communities therefore permits a preliminary identification of internal factors that promote village viability.

With respect to the social origins of the settlers, Oren is a more homogeneous community than Shikma: whereas at Oren only three families spent considerable periods of time in urban settings, Shikma is equally divided between rural and urban members. Shikma's comparative heterogeneity is significant in at least two different ways. For one thing, cultural differences be-

tween the settlers present potential points for group crystallization and factional organization: insofar as persons with an urban
background look down upon their "country cousins" and the
villagers similarly look askance upon the city group, cultural
differences tend to be ritually magnified and socially divisive.
Such divisions did in fact exist: the urban settlers speak French,
consider themselves to be cultivated persons, and think of the
rural group as more boorish and simple. The fact that the village
factions were not mixed illustrates how cultural distinctions separated the community. These differences are also important since
they are related to different outlooks regarding a farming career.
As might be expected, many urban settlers resisted farming and
did not become full time agriculturalists. On the other hand, the
rural immigrants adjusted more quickly to the new farming role.
These contrasts also promote opposition between factions; the
interests of the farmers and the non-farmers often clash. Thus,
not only may cultural heterogeneity lead to sharp differences
and schism, but the differences in specific cultural content also
leads to opposed outlooks and interests.

A second contrast between the villages consists in differences
in the range of social ties. At Oren, all but eight families had
some kinsmen in the village; in Shikma, on the other hand,
twenty-two families were without kin. This high proportion of
isolated families at Shikma lent the village its divided character.
The families did not become part of any integrative unit; there
was no group that offered them assistance or psychological support. These families did not take part in cooperative activities,
and therefore they tended to magnify the problem of attaining
village-wide consensus.

Oren and Shikma also differ in regard to the number and size
of factions. Shikma was split into four factions, while at Oren
two factional groups usually contested for power. Multiple factionalism at Shikma led to political instability and increased the
problem of attaining village-wide cooperation. The factional

groups at Oren were substantially larger than those at Shikma. For example, the Dehan faction normally included thirty families: fourteen of them were kinsmen, while the others were linked to the Dehans by friendship, common interest, and obligation. In 1958, the Dehan and Levi factions together included all but nine of Oren's fifty-seven families. The membership of these groups was relatively stable—a two-party system prevailed —and the factions have been able to institute long-term political control.

Finally, there were differences in the leadership structures of the two communities. At Oren the dominant village figures were the leaders of the larger kinship groups. These men found their main support from among their kinsmen and more generally from within the faction. They were therefore guaranteed a stable basis of support. At Shikma, on the other hand, the powerful leaders did not possess a guaranteed constituency. Paradoxically, neither of the two kinship-based factions had leaders who were able to assert general authority, while the two men with leadership abilities did not have the support of broadly based groups. This lack of balance between large constituencies and powerful leaders intensified village instability.

Thus far we have shown how Oren and Shikma differed in internal composition and organization. As was earlier indicated, the patterns of growth in these villages have been significantly different. Three main indices measure differences in development between them: the rate of migration, the degree of agricultural exploitation, and the stability of village-wide institutions. These indices refer to key features of village life, and, moreover, they render objectively determined expressions of community growth.

Oren and Shikma contrast sharply along these three dimensions. More families left Shikma than Oren: between 1954 and 1961 twenty-eight families moved from Shikma, whereas, between 1955 and 1961, nineteen families left Oren. The migration

was continuous from Shikma: the exodus extended through
1961, while at Oren the population hardly changed after 1957.
Defined in terms of migration, Oren was therefore a more stable
community than Shikma.

There are differences too in agricultural exploitation.[1] All of
the settlers at Oren farmed their land: as was indicated earlier in
this chapter, the villagers extended their range of farm work and
also seem to have become more expert. At Shikma, however,
nineteen of the forty-eight settlers did not work their farms;
more than a third of the villagers were employed outside of the
village (mainly as unskilled laborers). Those settlers who did
farm received crop yields similar to those at neighboring Oren;
in both villages some farmers obtained excellent results, while
others received average yields. Yet the villages were clearly
differentiated in regard to the numbers actively engaged in
farming.

Shikma and Oren also contrast in regard to the permanence of
community-wide institutions. At Oren, committee elections
were held once a year: between 1959 and 1961 two committees
were chosen and each served a year's term. During this same period at Shikma, seven different committees were chosen: elections were held several times each year, and personnel and
policies changed. Shikma was an inchoate, sharply divided community, while Oren developed relatively stable community institutions.

These differences between Oren and Shikma are summarized
in Table 6.

This table illustrates well the opposite characters of the villages:
Oren and Shikma differ in each category. However, Table 6

[1] Computing these differences poses many problems. There are small
differences in size, area, and crops between villages; comparison based
upon gross income or production is therefore difficult. Some proportion
of the harvests were not marketed cooperatively and therefore cannot be
accurately assessed. For these reasons, I have chosen to compare the
villages in regard to the number of persons actually engaged in farming.

does not indicate the relationships between the various factors. What are the factors in Oren's social composition which influenced its more positive growth? More specifically, if the first four categories in the table (origins, kinship, factional dominance, symmetric leadership) are taken as independent variables and the latter three as dependent variables (numbers leaving, agricultural exploitation, stability of village institutions), what are the relationships between them? What factors or combinations of factors led to diversity in types of communities?

Table 6. Comparison of Oren and Shikma

Name	Origins	Kinship based	Dominant factions	Symmetric leadership	Migrate	Farm	Village institutions
Oren	Rural	Yes	Yes	Yes	Few	Many	Stable
Shikma	Mixed	No	No	No	Many	Few	Unstable

Several tentative hypotheses may first be offered. We may speculate that the greater rate of migration from Shikma was a result both of the settlers' urban background and of their lack of family ties in the village. People with extensive urban traditions are likely to have greater difficulty in adjusting to a small, farming community; moreover, those lacking family ties have fewer supports (both psychological and economic) within the village. The migration statistics in both villages support this hypothesis. Twenty-six of the twenty-eight persons leaving Shikma had urban backgrounds; these same individuals were also characterized by a lack of family connections in the village. On the other hand, it will be recalled that the Oren settlers stemmed mainly from rural regions and that many people migrated because they had relatives there. We would predict, therefore, that Moroccan villages composed of settlers with urban backgrounds and without family ties would have a higher migration rate.

Similarly, the same two factors may account for the differences in farming between the villages. Urban persons are more likely to resist farming; for them the transition to a farming career is more problematic than for rural immigrants. Membership in large family groups has advantages for successful farming: kinship provides a sense of security, and it offers advantages with regard to cooperation in work. Of the nineteen settlers at Shikma who did not farm their land, seventeen were classed as urbanites; these same persons also lacked family ties in the community.

Stability of village institutions, the third dependent variable, is determined by factional size and by the structure of village leadership. The hypothesis is that villages which have dominant factions led by powerful leaders will have stable village institutions, whereas villages divided among rival factions and warring leaders are unable to develop stable village-wide bodies. According to this formulation, large factions permit a stable base for government; if these factions are led by powerful leaders, some measure of stability may obtain. On the other hand, if the factions are small, and if powerful leaders have no permanent source of support, the community becomes splintered and is unable to function successfully.

A testing of these hypotheses requires additional comparative material. The comparison between Oren and Shikma was particularly advantageous: both villages shared the same ecology, were settled at the same time, and included persons stemming from the same cultural area. Moreover, in both villages intensive village studies had been carried out. Several studies have also been undertaken recently in other Moroccan villages.[2] Although these data are more limited, they do permit a rough, tentative test. The comparison is not meant to be complete or statistically significant—the sample is much too small for fully systematic comparison. However, the additional material does

[2] Research reports on these villages were prepared by Z. Stup, R. Rehat, and M. Minkovitz. I benefited greatly from their reports and from conversations with them.

permit a preliminary checking of hypotheses and also indicates a general typology of *moshav* development.[3]

Five villages are introduced in this comparison. Table 7 shows the distribution of all the communities according to geographic area and year established.

Table 7. Moroccan villages according to region and age

Name	Region	Year founded
Oren	Negev	1954
Shikma	Negev	1953
Rommema	Negev	1957
Olar	Lachish	1955
Dvir	Lachish	1955
Asor	Lachish	1950
Magan	North	1950

This comparison increases the range of potential variables. The villages are distributed over a large area and their ecologic positions differ. For example, Magan is located near Haifa, a large urban center, but none of the other villages is situated near a city. Asor and Dvir, in the Lachish region, are adjoining communities, while Olar is situated in a different zone in Lachish. The villages in the Negev and Lachish area utilize the same crop schedule: vegetables and industrial crops form the basis of their

[3] A different view of *moshav* development is proposed in several studies published by members of the Sociology Department of the Hebrew University. Unlike the present study, which examines several villages in detail, the material that forms the basis of their studies was assembled by interviewing immigrants in a larger sample of villages. The presentation and analysis of their data also follows somewhat more formal lines, although some of the conclusions reached in their studies are similar to those presented in this book. Taken together, these studies present an interesting counterpoint of research in social anthropology and sociology. See D. Weintraub and M. Lissak, "Problems of Absorption of North African Immigrants in Small-holders' Cooperative Settlements in Israel," *Jewish Journal of Sociology*, III, No. 2 (1961); and Dov Weintraub, "A Study of New Farmers in Israel," *Sociologica Ruralis*, IV, No. 1 (1964).

crop rotations. Magan, however, has a program that combines
dairying and vegetable production. Furthermore, the villages are
affiliated with three different settlement movements: Oren,
Shikma, Magan, and Olar belong to the same socialist-oriented
confederation; Rommema and Dvir are affiliated with a religious
moshav group; and Asor is a member of a smaller, Liberal Party
affiliated movement. The ages of the villages are also different:
two villages (Asor and Magan) were formed during the first
wave of settlement, four others were established in 1954 and
1955 (Shikma, Oren, Olar, and Dvir), while Rommema was
founded in 1957.

While these differences in ecology, crop rotation, age, and political affiliation do complicate the comparison, a number of factors are common to all of the villages. In each one, all (or nearly
all) of the settlers immigrated from Morocco: although there
are regional differences among them, they all share a Moroccan
background. The age groups within each village are roughly
similar; each community includes a similar proportion of persons
of all age groups (See Table 8.) The *moshav* framework is

Table 8. Age distribution of villages

Age	Oren M F	Shikma M F	Rommema M F	Olar M F	Dvir M F	Asor M F	Magan M F
0–5	48 26	82	36 14	91 63	56 59	34 36	34 29
6–13	39 42	45 42	10 15	49 44	51 34	36 32	49 34
14–17	11 9	13 12	4 5	12 7	14 11	11 6	13 16
18–25	19 25	11 13	9 14	27 36	28 30	30 15	25 19
26–35	27 20	15 18	11 10	34 27	27 20	16 20	20 21
36–45	14 12	15 12	8 8	18 12	20 13	20 11	16 19
46–55	11 9	9 6	6 5	4 8	5 12	7 10	15 4
56–	8 8	5 2	4 0	13 4	10 5	6 1	4 14

common to them all; in every village community life is modeled
after the classic *moshav*. Finally, all of the villages were formed
and subsequently directed by the Settlement Department. These
similarities in composition and community organization enable

one to make meaningful, if limited, comparisons between communities.

A comparison of all seven villages indicates that they differ widely in regard to social composition and organization and also that their internal development varies systematically. Table 9 summarizes the variables.

Table 9. Comparison of Moroccan villages

Name	Origins	Kinship based	Dominant factions	Symmetric leadership	Migrate	Farm	Village institutions
Oren	Rural	Yes	Yes	Yes	Few	Many	Stable
Shikma	Mixed	No	No	No	Many	Few	Unstable
Rom- mema	Rural	Yes	No	Yes	Few	Few	Unstable
Olar	Rural	Yes	Yes	Yes	Few	Many	Stable
Dvir	Mixed	No	No	No	Many	Few	Unstable
Asor	Rural	Yes	No	No	Many	Many	Unstable
Magan	Urban	Yes	Yes	Yes	Few	Many	Stable

An analysis of the combinations of factors in this table leads to several conclusions. The wider comparisons tend to support the hypotheses suggested earlier. The hypothesis that village population stability is related to rural origins and extensive kinship groups is confirmed in four of the five new cases. In three of the four villages classed positively for these characteristics (Rommema, Olar, and Magan) comparatively few persons migrated.[4] Conversely, the village classed as mixed and lacking kinship groups (Dvir) is characterized by a high rate of leaving. One village, Asor, is an exception to this pattern: although the village contains both positive features, the rate of departure has been high. Asor's special development will be discussed at greater

[4] Only six of the original thirty families left Rommema. Thirty-seven families left Olar, most of them during the first year after their settlement, however. At Magan, fifteen settlers moved away during the first year and since then nine more. From Asor forty-two settlers left in a constant exodus. Fifty-seven settlers left Dvir; there, too, the rate of departure was constant.

length below. Meanwhile, one may conclude that the hypothesis receives general confirmation.

Similarly, the hypothesis that the adoption of a farming role is positively related to rural backgrounds and kinship affiliations receives support. Villages with a high proportion of farmers (Olar, Asor, and Magan) include rural persons and are kinship-based, and those with few farmers (Dvir) tend to have the opposite characteristics. Again, one village does not follow this pattern: Rommema is rural and includes kinsmen, but the villagers have not become farmers.

Both of these hypotheses are confirmed by a majority of cases. The third hypothesis—that stable village institutions are positively related to factional dominance and symmetric leadership —is supported by all cases: when both these factors are positive (Magan and Olar) the community possesses stable institutions; when both factors are negative (Dvir and Asor) village institutions are unstable; and when only one of the characteristics is present (Rommema), then, too, village institutions are unstable. These data support the notion that these factors are important conditions for the emergence of stable village institutions.

While the comparison does confirm the hypotheses in a general way, it does not allow a more precise focusing of relationships. In each instance, two variables are related to certain community features: which of the two factors is dominant, or what their relationships are, is not clarified by the comparison. For this reason, the possibility of refining the hypotheses is limited. There is one exception, however. Unlike the other villages, Magan is composed of urban settlers who are members of several kinship clusters. In all of the other cases, urban immigrants are not organized into larger primary groups. Magan has, moreover, developed in a "positive" fashion. Stability of the population, as well as the adjustment to farming, would therefore seem to depend mainly upon membership in kinship groups, rather than upon place of origin. This conclusion seems reasonable: kinship involves psychological support, and it also tends to be related to economic and political cooperation. It is likely, too, that the two variables have a different importance at various times in a settler's adjustment: place of origin and the related predispositions to change may dominate during the initial adjustment period, but at later stages family ties become increasingly important.

In most of the villages summarized in Table 9 the four independent variables appear in like combination: that is, they are all either positive or negative. Rommema and Dvir are variations on this theme: some variables are positive and others negative. These communities have also developed differently from the others. It will be useful to describe some features of the two variants at greater length.

Rommema's history contains a number of special features. All of the settlers had lived together in the same south-Moroccan village; this case is an instance of a village that was literally transplanted. In 1955 this community, which numbered some eighty families, emigrated as a group to Israel, and were resettled intact in a *moshav* in the northern region. Almost as soon as they arrived in the *moshav*, however, a series of violent internal difficulties broke out. The main source of dissension seems to have been a continuing struggle for community dominance: old rivalries as well as new problems contributed to create conditions of intense conflict. As a result of these tensions, several groups soon left the village: this transplanted community had, in effect, disintegrated in the new Israeli conditions.

One group of thirty families left the original *moshav* and took up residence at the then vacant Rommema. The composition of this migrating group is particularly interesting: the thirty families were divided into three kinship units comprising ten families each. This equal division does not seem to have been fortuitous, but was carefully planned by the settlers before they left for Rommema. The settlers recalled that before leaving for the new village they met informally and decided to migrate together only on condition that no group would be in the majority; rather, they would be of equal size and would have equal strength. They reasoned that no single group would be able to dominate the others and that all would have an equal voice in affairs. This balancing of population was more or less maintained, though three families later left the village and several young people applied to join the community.

Equality in factional size had a determining influence upon Rommema's development. In effect, it paralyzed the growth of community-wide institutions. From its very inception, the village was unable to elect a committee or secretary: at every election each faction supported its own leaders, and since the votes were inevitably equal, no decisions were made. Similarly, it was not possible to reach agreement on any phase of village policy. Problems were met by divided opinion, and the lack of consensus prevented decision making. These conditions also affected the adoption of farming. None of the settlers at Rommema farmed their land; they were all employed in various types of work in the village or the region. This reluctance to undertake farming stemmed from many factors. Principal among them, however, was the fact that the villagers were unable to agree upon policy: since they could not reach agreement, it was not possible to undertake community-wide cooperative activities. If some of the settlers decided to farm, the lack of cooperation on the part of others would make the attempt difficult.

The directions of growth at Asor are also of interest. Table 9 lists Asor as a community including rural elements and kin groups but lacking dominant factions and symmetric leadership. Two of the independent variables are positive and two negative. Factional organization in the village is of particular interest; indeed, this factor seems to have dominated the others. Asor was divided among three factions; none was large enough to constitute a majority, and, in fact, the three together did not include a majority of villagers. This division is reminiscent of Shikma; there, too, the village was divided among various small factions. Unlike Shikma, however, two of the factions at Asor were firmly tied to rival Israeli political parties. The largest faction (which included sixteen members) was bound to the party with which the village was affiliated, while a smaller group of seven families was associated with a different, rival party. These ties were not temporary but rather lasted over a number of years. They strengthened the division between the two factions and regularly introduced extraneous issues into village affairs: the political conflicts created chaotic situations, and village life tended to deteriorate. At Asor, political-party-inspired factional conflict prevented the positive development of village life.

Earlier, we noted how administrative reform might stimulate rapid change in new *moshavim:* the credit reform at Oren led to widespread patterns of change. This comparison of villages shows, however, that the possibility of rapid change varies greatly among communities and depends primarily upon internal village features. That is, whether or not a *moshav* is receptive to change and whether it is able to assimilate innovations successfully depends upon such factors as the size and number of village factions, the social origins of the settlers, or the extent of primary group ties. Variables such as these help to explain Oren's relative success in farming and village organization, and conversely, to explain why the neighboring Shikma remained disorganized. To a considerable degree, these variables are not easily manipulated: factions, for example, are generated by factors such as loyalty to kin or leaders, and administrators are unable to control or limit their growth. In general, then, while administrative reforms may have great impact, these reforms operate within rather narrow limits. Particular reforms may lead to change when internal village conditions are favorable, but the main variables influencing change lie in the community's sociopolitical structure. To succeed, administrative changes need to be tailored to suit the particular structure of each community.

The Oren-Shikma contrast well illustrates this point. The Department's new credit policy was introduced in both villages. At Shikma, however, it caused an immediate village crisis and was initially rejected. The village leaders strongly opposed the plan. They saw that the new program would remove authority from their hands: funds would no longer be distributed by the committee, and they would thereby lose a major source of power. Furthermore, the many unsuccessful farmers feared that the new system would be harsher than the earlier one and that they would suffer as a consequence. The settlers reacted violently, and for several months, Shikma was torn by conflict. Later, after long negotiation and argument, the plan was finally accepted. It is as yet unclear what results the new program will have at Shikma. It does not seem, however, as if the results will be as deep-seated and dramatic as they were at Oren.

Several other conclusions are indicated by this village comparison. It is best, however, to consider them in a wider focus. The analysis presented in this chapter identifies some of the variables leading to differences in village development. Oren has been placed in a somewhat larger perspective: historically, by a view of recent events in the village, and by a comparison of its growth with other Moroccan villages. However, Oren may be viewed in an even wider context: as an example of a community undergoing rapid, directed change. In this sense, Oren may be grouped with a larger range of communities. Administered community programs and village development projects have been initiated in recent years in a great many countries. These programs, such as India's massive village development scheme or smaller but comparable projects in Latin America and Africa, include both extensive village planning and some degree of administrative direction and control. Then, too, rapid change of an undirected kind has taken place in a great variety of tribal and peasant communities.[5] How is Oren's experience relevant to the general study of cultural change? What lessons may be gleaned from this attempt to establish new communities and to direct their development?

There are, to begin with, several conclusions of a methodological kind. Studying an administered community—a community directed by outside, bureaucratically organized agencies—is obviously much different from studying a tribal or peasant society. Whereas, among the latter, anthropologists have been able to comprehend and analyze a community as if it were self-contained, one cannot successfully study an administered group without analyzing social units external to the community itself. Since the unfolding of events within the administered community depends upon the decisions and activities of the administrators, their modes of organization, as well as their outlook and behavior, must be carefully examined. This point seems simple enough, and yet it extends anthropological inquiry into areas somewhat removed from traditional studies. What is more, to understand social processes within such a community, one must understand how political parties, or other national and regional agencies, influence events within the community. In short, the entire social field needs to be studied, and, therefore, the analyst must pursue his inquiries both within the community and within those groups outside of the village which become significant in the daily course of village life. This task is surely possible, but it demands widening the usual anthropological focus.

A second note on method relates to the length of time required for such studies. To understand the development process in communities of this type, it is necessary to make systematic observations over a considerable period of time. Conditions

[5] See S. C. Dube, *India's Changing Villages: Human Factors in Community Development* (London: Routledge and Kegan Paul, 1958) or Margaret Mead, *New Lives for Old* (New York: W. Morrow and Company, 1956).

change rapidly—this is a hallmark of administered communities
—and the tempo and direction of village growth may therefore
take new and unexpected directions. Thus, for example, the
third stage in Oren's growth was not predicted by events in the
previous stage: had my observations come to a close in, say,
1959, the prognosis would likely have been for a continued state
of village crisis, factional dispute, and general disaffection. Additional time was needed to observe how events ultimately unfolded. To study rapidly changing situations, then, one needs
observations extending beyond the normal research period of a
year or eighteen months, so that events constantly in flux may
arrive at some resolution. Without such a time span, observations and conclusions are likely to be only partially accurate or
even entirely misleading.

To turn next to a general interpretation of the events considered in this study, the very scope and rapidity of change is a
striking feature of Oren's brief history: yesterday's artisans and
peddlers are today's farmers and co-workers. One way of explaining this development is to note the positive relationship
between totally new conditions and rapid change. The Oren experience indicates that, given entirely new social and cultural conditions, rapid change is possible. Several reasons may be cited for
this relationship. Immigration separated people from their traditional social networks: long-standing patterns of family and
community authority were removed, and the potential for accepting change was therefore magnified. There were fewer
obstacles to bar or interfere with the adoption of new patterns
of behavior. The immigrants perceived that their former way of
life was not appropriate to their new life in Israel: settled in a
moshav, one simply could not continue to be a sandalmaker or
shopkeeper. They shared a sense of separation from the past—a
dramatic, deep break—and of the necessity to begin afresh.
They were typically responsive to change and were disposed to

accept at least certain features of the new social and cultural environment.

These conclusions are pertinent to migrants and migrations in general. Veblen, for example, has remarked that the perception of changed conditions contributed to the speed with which many European peasant immigrants adjusted to an urban American factory system.[6] In that instance, too, conditions were totally different, and the obvious break with the past encouraged the acceptance of a new technology as well as new modes of behavior. Of course, this does not apply to all immigrant groups; some, such as the Amish in America or religious *chassidic* groups in Israel, self-consciously seek to maintain earlier traditions and attempt to perpetuate a traditional social and cultural environment.[7] As was emphasized in the previous chapter, the Moroccan settlers at Oren maintained important cultural traditions and reinterpreted significant portions of their new social environment. Change was not complete and all-embracing but rather selective and partial. Then, too, the break with the past does not explain the differences in development between Moroccan *moshavim*—between Oren and Shikma, for example. Other factors explain the contrasts in community development. Yet, these qualifications notwithstanding, the entrance into a new social universe and the general sense of necessity to adapt to a new way of life do help to explain the rapidity of change at Oren.

Settlement in a *moshav* represented a complete cultural change. The immigrants left one cultural design—a life typified, for example, by residence in the *millah*, artisan or shopkeeper occupations, Moroccan Jewish speech and dress, uncertain ties

[6] T. Veblen, *The Portable Veblen*, ed. by Max Lerner (New York: Viking, 1948).

[7] W. M. Kollmorgen, "The Agricultural Stability of the Old Order Amish and Old Order Mennonites of Lancaster County, Pennsylvania," *American Journal of Sociology*, XLIX (1943), 233–241.

with the Muslims—and later, in the *moshav,* adopted a completely different cultural pattern. New commodities or types of social organization were not introduced gradually, while traditional patterns were maintained; instead, the entire pattern was changed, as it were, all at once. New groups were formed; farming careers were begun immediately, a new language, diet, and dress were adopted. There were, in fact, few carry-overs from the older traditions. The abrupt shift to a totally new and very different way of life quickened the pace of change and enlarged its range as well.

The speculation is, then, that rapid change becomes possible under new social and cultural conditions and that what makes it possible is the adoption of an entirely new cultural design. This stress upon the significance of total change has also been recognized in other studies. For example, in *New Lives for Old,* Margaret Mead argues that rapid change is possible precisely when it is a change in total cultural pattern. "A contribution of the Manus experience," she writes, "is the suggestion that rapid change is not only possible, but may actually be desirable, that instead of advocating slow partial changes we should advocate that a people who choose to practice a new technology or enter into drastically new kinds of economic relations will do so more easily if they live in different houses, wear different clothes, and eat different foods." [8]

Mead's conclusion emphasizes the conditions necessary for rapid change and also its desirability. In regard to the latter, neither Mead's Manus data nor the Israeli material offers fully convincing proof of the desirability of rapid change. Whether rapid change is better than gradual shifts depends upon criteria for "better" and "worse" and also upon truly comparative tests. For example, there are no cases of Moroccan *moshavim* in which change was not total or where changes were introduced gradually rather than all at once. But, if the "desirability" aspects of

[8] Mead, *op. cit.,* pp. 445–446.

Mead's conclusion are not supported by the Israeli material, her more general hypothesis is confirmed. In Israel, as in Manus, rapid change seems to have occurred because the total cultural pattern shifted and because the shift was abrupt rather than gradual.

Unlike the Manus case, however, Oren is an example of *directed* change. Mead speaks of a people "who choose to practice" a new way of life. Do the Oren settlers fall within the category of communities which choose to reorganize their lives? Probably not. As has been emphasized throughout this study, the immigrants never chose to settle at Oren, never wished to become farmers, and certainly did not desire to live within a cooperative system. These changes were all imposed upon the settlers. In addition, the village was not autonomous but was directed from outside. Both of these conditions—the original imposition of a new social and cultural pattern, and the subsequent direction of village affairs—bear upon the role of choice in Oren's development.

It would seem that, under certain conditions, large-scale changes may be successfully imposed upon a community. To put it differently: it is not necessarily the case that choice is a prerequisite for rapid, extensive cultural change. This is a conclusion of general significance, particularly since it seems contrary to many previous studies of rapid cultural change. For example, in an article summarizing the conditions necessary for large-scale change, Norman Chance lists choice as a determining factor.[9] This hypothesis is repeated widely throughout the literature.[10] The logic of this position is that choice activates and commits community members to some given path, whereas coercion restrains community creativity and leads to resistance or

[9] Norman Chance, "Culture Change and Integration: An Eskimo Example," *American Anthropologist*, LXII (1960), 1041.

[10] See Manning Nash, *Machine Age Maya* (American Anthropological Association Memoir 87, 1958); and Robert Redfield, *Chan Kom: A Village That Chose Progress* (Chicago: University of Chicago Press, 1950).

apathy. Oren's experience seems to have been clearly to the contrary. Thus it would appear that large-scale reorganizations do not necessarily depend upon choice.

Under what conditions, then, may extensive changes be imposed upon communities? Several such conditions have already been suggested; a disposition to accept a new situation brought on by migration or other shifts in the social and cultural environment, and the availability of a totally different cultural design may be conditions for an imposed change. The very shock and strangeness of the new situation may encourage an inclination to accept guidance and submit to a wholly foreign way of life. Certainly the immigrants at Oren did not accept a new farming role because it expressed a continuation of their previous traditions or because it represented an old, repressed cultural dream; nothing could be further from the truth. They began farming because they were thrust into a totally novel situation and because they were disposed to accept the new circumstances.

Then, too, what appeared to be a lack of alternatives further conditioned the settlers' acceptance of their new life. They were brought directly to the village, and there seemed to be no option other than to accept conditions, however grudgingly. True, one might—and some did—leave the village; but migration was always a tedious, prolonged effort. Village authorities discouraged migration, and, since they controlled housing, they were able to limit the exodus. Forced to remain in the village, the settlers entered into the farming activities.

These remarks pertain most directly to the first group of immigrants, to those who were brought directly from ship to village. However, it will be recalled, other settlers later migrated to Oren; in effect, they chose to settle in a farming cooperative. Was their choice significant for their subsequent adjustment? Perhaps; many of those who chose Oren—such as the Dehan and Levi families—later became successful farmers. But so many different variables are related to their adoption of *moshav* life that no firm conclusions may be drawn. Moreover, since some of those who were brought, as well as some of those who chose to come, successfully adapted to *moshav* life, active choice in this case does not seem to be a precondition for rapid cultural change.

The discussion has thus far centered upon the imposition of a new way of life. However, village life was also directed by outside authorities. Community affairs were managed for the settlers. How did external direction influence the adoption of new cultural patterns?

Whereas the transfer to village life and the initiation into agriculture were rigid and unbending directives, and the management of daily affairs was dominated by the Department and village instructors, the plans themselves were often flexible and open to manipulation, and the settlers were also partially involved in the process of decision making. The settlers did not initiate or propose policies, but they were able to influence the Department's proposals. As was earlier pointed out, by practicing noncooperation the villagers had a virtual veto power over certain of the Department's schemes. The system was rarely authoritarian: the settlers could resist plans, and if their opposition was firm enough, they were likely to win an argument or negotiate a compromise. Punishing censures were rarely applied and then only for brief periods. Moreover, the Department itself often took a flexible, pragmatic view: if the settlers stoutly resisted some scheme, Department officials were usually ready to consult with them and to follow some other course. Communications and "feedback" between the settlers and the planners were close and continuous. Settlement planners, from national directors to regional instructors, visited the villages and were well informed regarding a community's mood and recent village events. Of course, the Department sometimes insisted upon implementing some scheme, or it failed to interpret the settlers' views properly. Nevertheless, while it was sometimes clumsy and lacking in coordination, the administrative apparatus was well informed and was often able to propose realistic alternatives.

Thus, while the initial immersion into a new sociocultural system was, in effect, sudden and complete, the system itself changed gradually. The Department revised some of its proposals—for example, the new credit plan described in this chapter—and the settlers were able to reinterpret portions of the *moshav* system. Once they were "within the system," it became possible to alter and adjust its details and some of the key structural features as well.

Then, too, the local village committee did participate in framing policy and was in fact a useful training ground for eventual local autonomy. The committee was, at first, little more than a fiction; it was a convenient forum for the village instructors, a setting for them to issue directives and hear grievances. In time, however, the settlers sensed the importance that the committee might have, and the more aggressive among them realized that they might use the committee in order to grasp control of the village. Involvement in local politics brought village leaders into contact with larger channels of influence and power: they sought to use the national press, appealed to political parties for support, and presented their arguments before national agricultural administrators. In brief, since it was possible to influence the system, the settlers became involved in it and, to some degree, committed to it. Oren was an administered community, but the system of administration permitted the influencing of policy and thereby led to the development of more appropriate plans, as well as the involvement of the settlers in directing events. New cultural patterns were adopted as more suitable plans were formulated and as the settlers, participating within the system, became engaged in the new way of life.

These comments regarding community direction may also apply to other programs of planned rural development. From the vantage point of the administrator, Oren's development underscores the importance of administrative systems that permit the villagers to influence and guide the planners' choice. A rare flexibility is needed: the administrator must have the ability to encourage discussion and opposition, and to frame new programs as the reasons for doubt or village opposition are better understood. Open communication is an obvious necessity for this relationship; only if the villagers are free to express their feelings and the planners are close enough to the community to understand its wishes is this type of direction likely to succeed.

Economic factors are further important components in Oren's cultural transformation. The Department's program of guidance was also a commitment of economic resources; imposing a technology it knew to be wholly foreign to the immigrants' traditions, the Department underwrote the new farmers' losses and guaranteed them a regular income. This economic security had a primary significance in Oren's development. Had the settlers been thrown upon their own resources, they undoubtedly would have failed and become increasingly discouraged and apathetic. Economic security provided a necessary cushion. Moreover, when the settlers became more economically independent, after the reform of the credit system, agricultural prices remained at a high level. This fortunate merging of events helped to sustain the settlers. These conclusions indicate that economic security may be beneficial for rapid change and that national planning groups may need to underwrite new ventures financially, with the expectation that their investments will be repaid much later, if at all.

Two other conditions for community development in a situation of directed change may be gleaned from the intervillage comparison. The retention of primary group ties seems especially significant. Generational and other tensions did disturb many family groups; but no attempt was made to alter or reorganize family relations. On the contrary, the *moshav* system emphasized the family. More important, kinship ties were reinforced, and the relations between kinsmen assumed new dimensions. Thus, the settlers' primary units of cooperation and emotional security were not damaged; this continuity in relations in a situation of widespread change undoubtedly contributed to the adoption of new cultural patterns. Had family life been reorganized—within a much different type of social system—the strains upon emotional security might well have led to despair and ultimate chaos.[11]

Village leadership is another important variable in the adoption of new patterns. Oren's leaders were not extraordinary men; they did not exhibit a genius for organization or unusual gifts of wisdom. They were, at best, competent, forceful, and willing to learn. Yet these very qualities—their skill in learning how the political system functioned, their ability to manipulate it, and their success in influencing their kinsmen and followers —are important components in Oren's development. Men such as Moshe Dehan or Shimon Levi quickly came to understand the new situation and were able to interpret it to others; they were able to convince their followers of their policies, and they could also manage affairs outside of the village. Their influence aided the adoption of new traditions, and their skills allowed the village to become increasingly autonomous.

Oren's experience indicates that directed change may be possible, and it reveals some of the variables that make such change possible. The relationships between these variables—leadership, new conditions, or a lack of alternatives—are still general and imprecise. Additional comparative studies are needed to understand these situations more fully. Still, the Israeli data present important evidence of how new communities are formed and developed and how new patterns of behavior are quickly

[11] Eisenstadt makes the same point in his analysis of immigrant villages. See S. N. Eisenstadt, "Sociological Aspects of the Economic Adaptation of Oriental Immigrants in Israel: A Case Study in the Process of Modernization," *Economic Development and Cultural Change*, IV, No. 3 (1956).

adopted. Oren's brief history may be a useful model for the examination of other programs of village development. Although distinctive in certain respects—particularly the settlers' lack of agricultural traditions—the Oren experience indicates some important patterns of village growth and change.

Bibliography

Abbou, I. *Musulmans, Andalous, et Judeo Espagnols*. Casablanca: Editions Antar, 1953.

Assaf, A. *The Moshav Ovdim in Israel* (in Hebrew). Tel Aviv: Moshav Movement Publications, 1953.

Ben Gurion, D. *Jewish Labour*. London: Hechalutz Organization of England, 1936.

Berlin, I. "The Origins of Israel," in *The Middle East in Transition*, ed. by W. Laquer. London: Routledge and Kegan Paul, 1958.

Borrie, W. D. *The Cultural Absorption of Immigrants*. Paris: UNESCO, 1959.

Chance, N. "Culture Change and Integration: An Eskimo Example," *American Anthropologist*, LXII (1960).

Chouraqui, A. *Les Juifs d'Afrique du Nord: Marche vers l'Occident*. Paris: Presses Universitaires de France, 1952.

——. "North African Jewry Today," *Jewish Journal of Sociology*, I (1959).

Dayan, S. *Moshav Ovdim*. Tel Aviv: Palestine Pioneer Library No. 6, 1947.

Dube, S. C. *India's Changing Villages: Human Factors in Community Development*. London: Routledge and Kegan Paul, 1958.

Eisenstadt, S. N. *The Absorption of Immigrants*. Glencoe: Free Press, 1955.

——. "Sociological Aspects of the Economic Adaptation of Oriental

Immigrants in Israel: A Case Study in the Process of Modernization," *Economic Development and Cultural Change*, IV, No. 3 (1956).

Goren, J. *The Villages of the New Immigrants in Israel, Their Organization and Management* (in Hebrew). Tel Aviv: Ministry of Agriculture, Agricultural Publications Division, 1960.

Goulven, J. *Les Mellahs de Rabat-Sale.* Paris: Editions Larose, 1923.

Halperin, H. *Changing Patterns in Israeli Agriculture.* London: Routledge and Kegan Paul, 1957.

Herskovits, M. *Cultural Anthropology.* New York: Knopf, 1955.

Houtsma, M. Th., *et al. The Encyclopedia of Islam.* Leyden: Brill, 1913–1936.

Israel Government Yearbook 5712 (1951/52). Jerusalem: The Government Printer.

Jacobs, M. *A Study of Culture Stability and Change: The Moroccan Jewess.* Washington: Catholic University Press, 1956.

Kollmorgen, W. M. "The Agricultural Stability of the Old Order Amish and Old Order Mennonites of Lancaster County, Pennsylvania," *American Journal of Sociology*, XLIX (1943).

Lehrman, H. "Morocco's Jews Enter the Twentieth Century," *Commentary*, XVIII (1954).

———. "Morocco's Jews Between Islam and France," *Commentary*, XX (1955).

Le Tourneau, R. *Fes avant le Protectorat.* Casablanca: SMLE Société Marocaine, 1949.

Levy, R. *The Social Structure of Islam.* Cambridge: Cambridge University Press, 1957.

Lindberg, S. *The Background to Swedish Migration.* Minneapolis: University of Minnesota Press, 1931.

The London Jewish Chronicle.

Malka, E. *Essai d'Ethnographie des Mellahs.* Rabat: Imperie Omnia, 1946.

Mead, M. *New Lives for Old.* New York: Morrow, 1956.

Mills, C. Wright. *The Puerto Rican Journey.* New York: Harpers, 1951.

Nash, M. *Machine Age Maya.* [Menasha, Wis.]: American Anthropological Association, 1958.

Navo, N. *Shikma: A Village in the Western Negev.* Jewish Agency, Settlement Department, mimeo, 1961.

Patai, R. *Israel Between East and West*. Philadelphia: Jewish Publication Society, 1953.

Petersen, W. *Planned Migration*. Berkeley and Los Angeles: University of California Press, 1955.

Price, C. A. "Immigration and Group Settlement," in W. D. Borrie, *The Cultural Absorption of Immigrants*. Paris: UNESCO, 1959.

Redfield, R. *Chan Kom: A Village That Chose Progress*. Chicago: University of Chicago Press, 1950.

Reinhold, H. *Youth Builds Its House* (in Hebrew). Tel Aviv, 1951.

Report of the 22nd World Zionist Congress (in Hebrew). Jerusalem: Jewish Agency, 1947.

Report of the 23rd World Zionist Congress (in Hebrew). Jerusalem: Jewish Agency, 1950.

Report of the 25th World Zionist Congress (in Hebrew). Jerusalem: Jewish Agency, 1955.

Sarfaty, A. "Yahas Fes," *Hesperis*, XIX (1934).

Shuval, J. "Patterns of Inter-group Tension and Affinity," *International Social Science Bulletin*, VIII, No. 1 (1956).

Spicer, E. *Human Problems in Technological Change*. New York: Russell Sage Foundation, 1952.

Spiro, M. *Kibbutz: Venture in Utopia*. Cambridge: Harvard University Press, 1956.

Statistical Abstract of Israel. Jerusalem: The Government Printer.

A Summary of Settlements Administered by the Settlement Department (in Hebrew). Jerusalem: Jewish Agency, Settlement Department, 1959.

Vajda, G. "Un Recueil de Textes Historiques Judeo Marocains," *Hesperis*, XXXV (1948), and XXXVI (1949).

Veblen, T. *The Portable Veblen*, ed. by Max Lerner. New York: Viking, 1948.

Voinot, L. *Pelerinages Judeo-Musulmans du Maroc*. Paris: Larose, 1949.

Weingarten, M. *Life in a Kibbutz*. New York: Reconstructionist Press, 1955.

Weingrod, A. "Change and Continuity in a Moroccan Immigrant Village in Israel," *Middle East Journal*, XIV (1960).

——. "Moroccan Jewry in Transition" (in Hebrew), *Megamot*, IX (1960).

——. "Administered Communities: Some Characteristics of New

Immigrant Villages in Israel," *Economic Development and Cultural Change*, XI (1962).

——. "Reciprocal Change: A Case Study of a Moroccan Immigrant Village in Israel," *American Anthropologist*, LXIV (1962).

——. "The Two Israels," *Commentary*, XXX (1962).

——. *Israel: A Study in Group Relations*. New York: Praeger, 1965.

Weintraub, D. "A Study of New Farmers in Israel," *Sociologica Ruralis*, IV (1964).

—— and M. Lissak. "Problems of Absorption of North African Immigrants in Small-Holders Cooperative Settlements in Israel," *Jewish Journal of Sociology*, III (1962).

Willner, D. "Politics and Change in Israel: The Case of Land Settlement," *Human Organization*, XXIV (1965).

Index